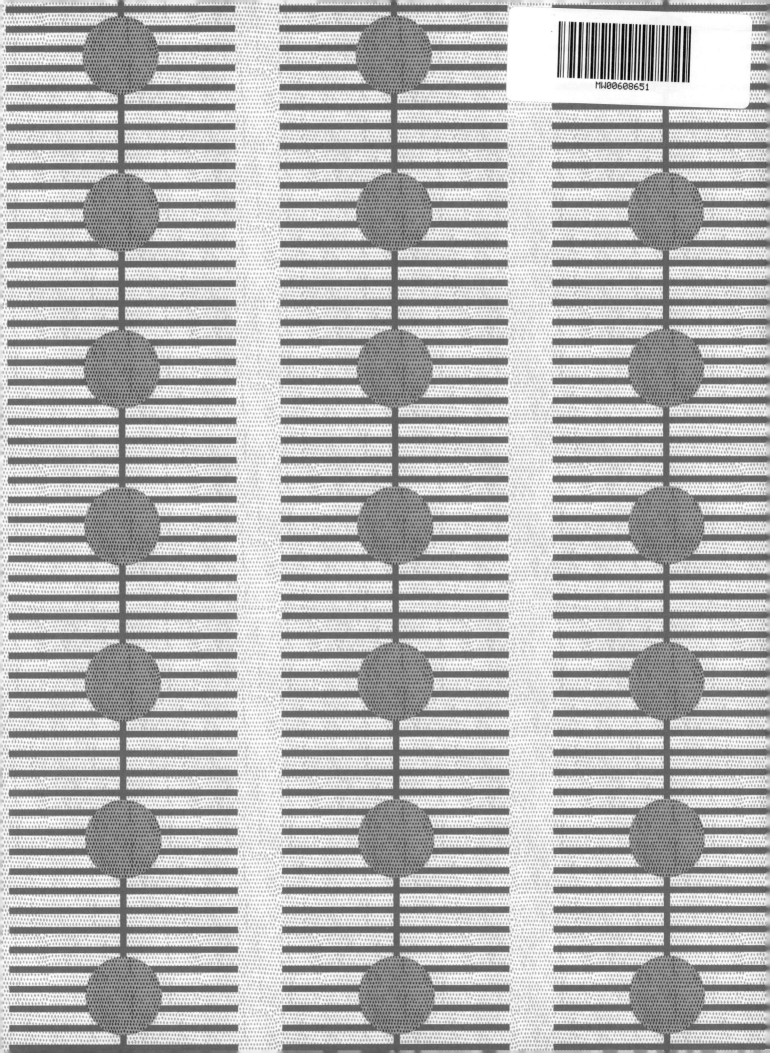

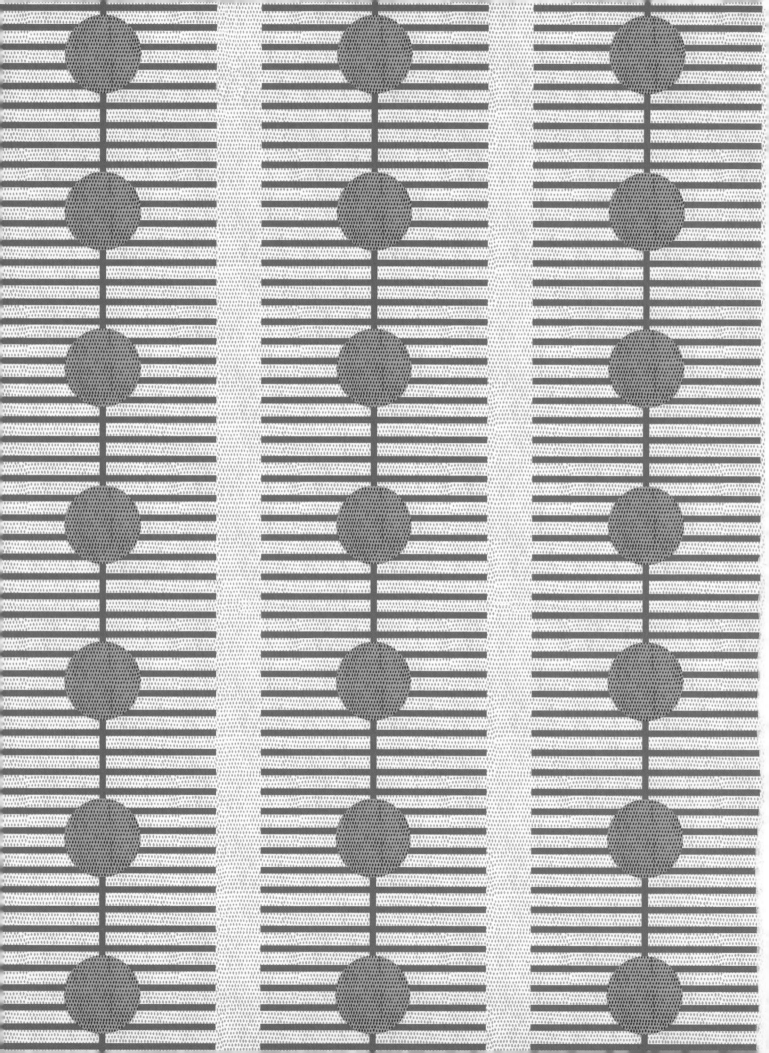

ICONIC HOME

ICONIC HOME

INTERIORS, ADVICE, AND STORIES FROM 50 AMAZING BLACK DESIGNERS

BY **JUNE REESE**

FOREWORD BY AMY ASTLEY

ABRAMS, NEW YORK

Contents

Foreword

In your hands you are holding a significant volume, a formidable collection of some of today's most talented Black designers. Whatever your personal style, page after page, I guarantee you will be as wowed as I am and find yourself captivated by each profile. As a whole, this dreamy portfolio of inspiring interiors offers a master class on why these talented tastemakers are at the top of their game.

When the Black Interior Designers Network approached *Architectural Digest* several years ago with the idea for the Iconic Home show house, we were thrilled to share our significant platforms to help draw more and much-deserved attention to the talents featured within. Many from that first showcase and those that followed are now celebrated in this very compendium and, like all fifty stars in this book, have gone on to create some of the most dynamic private homes and spaces around the world.

I am energized by all of the creativity and vision displayed here in *Iconic Home*, and I hope you feel it, too. How exciting to celebrate beauty wherever we see it.

— AMY ASTLEY

global editorial director and US editor in chief,
Architectural Digest

Introduction

"If you're reading this book, I share with you the gift of courage, tenacity, and the importance of making the uncomfortable decisions and choosing to forge your own path in life."

June Reese

Many years ago, I sat in my childhood living room fumbling my way through the finishes of Chief Architect, an architecture software program, adding wall coverings, bold patterns, and textures to the home model my boyfriend had created in a class he was taking. At the time, designing an interior seemed very insignificant. Later, design would become a source of joy and the path to a life I'd only dreamed of (long before I genuinely understood my own purpose). I've been in the design industry for over a decade now, and today I stand in awe of the many opportunities design has presented to me, but few are more welcome than the opportunity to create this book.

I often think about the girl I was, who struggled through high school, was not afforded the opportunity to be formally exposed to what would become a passion, and was unsure of her next steps just months before graduation. With no acceptances to any of my preferred journalism programs, I deferred to almighty Google to determine a viable career path. What I'd believed to be pure luck or coincidence at the time, I now understand was fate. For a young Black girl in a rural Texas town, there were not many career paths promoted to me, close to zero of which were in the arts. Contrary to popular belief, a profitable and sustainable career in art *is* possible when access and education are provided.

Like most spaces that are lacking in diversity, design school was uncomfortable and a culture shock for me. The weight of a full load of college courses—all while navigating my twenties—even led to me to consider changing careers. Then I was introduced to Kimberly Ward, designer and founder of the Black Interior Designers Network, and the passion I first felt for interior design was reignited.

Throughout the last seven years, I have met and spoken with Black designers from all over the globe. Learning that my experiences were not singular was both freeing and troubling. Taking inventory of the many conversations, I realized that the majority of designers had a very similar story that led to their careers. From this realization, the book *Iconic Home* was born. Through comprehen-

sive interviews, I unraveled the design philosophies and influential experiences that contribute to the breathtaking interiors we love.

Curating only fifty out of the many talented Black interior designers working today was not an easy task, but I've truly found pride in being able to build the monumental rarity that this book represents for the industry. In addition to their individual stories and experiences, each designer in the book has shared their wisdom and the design process they use to produce beautiful interiors. I hope that you can use the knowledge presented in these pages in your own home to create spaces that foster wellness, a better quality of life, and the sense of safety you deserve.

While *Iconic Home* celebrates some of today's most talented Black interior designers, it's also meant to serve as a symbol of encouragement and comfort to my younger self and to young people everywhere. Though it may not be clear now because you lack resources or support, one day you'll know exactly who you are, what your purpose is, and what your legacy will be.

If you're reading this book, I share with you the gift of courage, tenacity, and the importance of making the uncomfortable decisions and choosing to forge your own path in life. Remember, your goals and dreams are your own. Always go with your gut, challenge fear, and follow your dreams.

And by all means, be ICONIC.

After Leah Alexander graduated from college in San Diego, California, she moved to Los Angeles and sought the help of a recruiter to begin a career she might not otherwise have had access to. The recruiter helped her land an interior design job in West Hollywood, and she hasn't looked back since.

Leah now runs her own design firm, Beauty Is Abundant, and uses a signature mix of bold color and pattern in each room her team transforms. "Oftentimes, I find that the spaces [I design] end up with a neon heart," she says. "Somehow, organically, a pop of color is what completes the work—whether in the form of a large artwork, a vibrant backsplash, a bold rug, or an unusual accent chair. Without it, I feel spaces can fall flat."

Why is it important to layer a room design?
Layering makes inhabitants in a space feel enveloped, swathed, insulated from excess external stimuli. I love layering lighting with three or four light sources per room for mood and function.

What about texture?
I love texture. It breaks up monotony. It typically feels nice under hand or underfoot and allows us to flex our design muscles by encouraging color-shy clients to try something they otherwise may not have [tried] in textures and patterns. Texture in art—for example, with framed tapestries or plaster wall sculptures—is a unique way bring depth and variety to a room. Jute or rattan light fixtures add a textural element in a less obvious way than a throw blanket or pillow, which are also ways to add texture, especially when mixing fabrics and weaves.

"I love layering lighting with three or four light sources per room for mood and function."

Leah Alexander

This modern farmhouse dining room is fitted with organic and sleek modern lines complemented by warm, earthy tones. Designed for a *New York Times* bestselling author transitioning from New York to Atlanta.

"My work is deeply rooted in supporting diversity in the design community by collaborating with underrepresented artists and vendors who contribute talent, culture, and worldviews alongside us."

How does being a Black designer influence your work?

Being a Black designer with West Indian, Southern Californian, and most recently, Atlantan influences makes for dynamic, modern, vibrant design work. My work is deeply rooted in supporting diversity in the design community by collaborating with underrepresented artists and vendors who contribute talent, culture, and worldviews alongside us.

Is scale a factor in your designs?

Scale is so important. Too-small nightstands are a personal pet peeve. I like to see a minimum of a 30-inch-wide nightstand for king-size beds and larger. Chests as nightstands are great options beside Eastern king-size, California king, or any similarly massive size bed. I've had a couple of primary bedrooms that were so large they were studies in scale, zoning, and proportion. For those, my team used three-drawer chests as nightstands. Large area rugs, art, and light fixtures help put large spaces into perspective.

What about focal points?

I love a good focal point (that isn't a TV). Artwork, wall sculptures, wallpaper, light fixtures, fireplaces, picture windows, and enormous indoor trees all serve as wonderful focal points.

Do you have a design philosophy or something that you go by as a designer?

My design philosophy is in my firm's name. Beauty is abundant. There's beauty in spaces before we begin working on them, from the hard work our clients did to obtain them to the beautiful fact that we're being entrusted with them. There's beauty in mistakes that we'll hopefully learn from and avoid in the future. We inject this philosophy into our relationships with our clients and with each other, with the hope that we all take this way of being into the world every day.

What do you want people to remember about you?

I want our former, current, and future clients, people in general, and most importantly, you, the person reading this, to remember that we are reflections of one another and that your beauty is abundant.

OPPOSITE TOP LEFT: Transitional dining nook with modern accents. OPPOSITE TOP RIGHT: A Georgia playroom for two energetic boys with crazy cool parents who love art, colors, music, learning, and playing. The room is enameled in Sherwin-Williams Rayo de Sol yellow paint, with a clean and modern play table from Crate & Barrel as the epicenter of creativity. OPPOSITE BOTTOM LEFT: Instrument gallery featuring a custom ceramic planter created by the client. OPPOSITE BOTTOM RIGHT: Modern and playful powder room with Sherwin-Williams Enticing Red on the ceiling and art by Tafui.

Elliott Barnes's career began as an architect with Arthur Erickson Architects in Los Angeles. He would later switch to a focus on interiors when he moved to Paris to work with Andrée Putman. Since then Barnes has designed luxurious spaces all over the world. When designing, Elliott follows his "funneling" approach to a project. "I begin by defining the larger whole, which sets up the framework for individual expressions of the smaller parts," says Barnes. "Empathy is essential. When one is empathic, it is truly possible to create memorable work for others."

While designing, Elliott often applies his architectural background in unexpected ways. His use of lighting and contrast sets the tone for many of his projects. "I strive to create an architectural lighting that is about the orchestration of light and shadows to enhance the forms and surfaces of a space. I also utilize contrast, as it is important to provide accents to highlight or to provoke emotion. I usually establish a baseline or backdrop with one type of expression and then install another opposing expression when I want to emphasize a certain moment or highlight a certain detail."

In addition, his passion for the arts is amplified by the development of his collection, The Barnes Contemporary, a nonprofit that supports artists across the African diaspora. The collection showcases art across a series of spaces while developing a narrative about the collector and their collection. "It permits my clients to tell their own story," he notes.

How do you bring the outdoors in with your designs?

In my opinion, it starts by opening up the wall to the outside as much as possible and by continuing the floor material from the outside to the inside. If possible, I also insert a built-in architectural mirror

"Exaggerated changes in scale allow me to accentuate moments of transition or emphasize ideas of monumentality or intimacy."

Elliott Barnes

Elliott Barnes drew inspiration for this Dom Ruinart–themed living room from the oldest champagne house, Maison Ruinart. The designer sourced local materials to integrate the overall calmness of the home's location. The fireplace mantel is an original eighteenth-century one, which is elevated with a low table designed by Elliott.

> *"I don't install art on a wall or in a space so that the space looks better. I choose to install art in specific places because the work may be appreciated better in that location."*

or place a large decorative mirror on the wall opposing the windows so that the outside is reflected on the inside.

Why is scale important in design?
Exaggerated changes in scale allow me to accentuate moments of transition or emphasize ideas of monumentality or intimacy—for example, using an extra-small door to enter a larger room to emphasize the bigger volume, or making a large opening in a small wall to bring two spaces together.

Do you have a design philosophy you go by?
Two things guide me. One was given to me by an older student when I was studying architecture: "K.I.S.S.—keep it simple, stupid." And another quote I read from Antoine de Saint-Exupéry when I began my career in Paris: "A designer knows he has achieved perfection not when there is nothing left to add but when there is nothing left to take away."

How does art impact a space?
There is design and then there is art. Art lives its own life. I don't install art on a wall or in a space so that the space looks better. I choose to install art in specific places because the work may be appreciated better in that location. It's about highlighting the art, not the design. Many times, the placement of art is fluid, because I know that the clients will hang different works in the same location according to the evolution of their collection.

How do you think of functionality?
I am a true believer in the Louis Sullivan statement, "Form follows function." Functionality is the backbone of all successful designs. It's about designing with a purpose and an intent directly related to and as a result of a project's function, or the way a space or an object will be used.

What about movement?
Movement through a space or series of spaces is directly related to the way in which I want a project to be discovered. I often modulate volumes, axes, and light to create a *promenade architecturale*. My own projects are based on the Le Corbusier principle of "une promenade architecturale," a principle or primary circuit or path that orchestrates movement through spaces to provide moments of symmetry and asymmetry, moments of light and dark, moments of focus and panorama, and moments of transition and pause. It allows the discovery of multiple connected spaces as in a story or film.

OPPOSITE TOP: Minimalist living room in Paris featuring a custom table by Christian Liaigre and artwork by Huang Yan. OPPOSITE BOTTOM: In this luxurious bedroom, a limewash on the walls creates a soft contrast with the minimalist custom headboard. A custom folding screen and chair by Frédéric Sicard separates the lounging area from the open en suite bathroom.

"Texture is how we push forward or pull back certain colors in a space."

Arianne Bellizaire

When designing a space, Arianne Bellizaire leads with a focus on return on investment (ROI) for each and every client that works with her design firm. Since launching in 2013, her Louisiana-based design firm has transformed both residential and commercial spaces, striking a balance between client wants and functionality. Arianne describes interiors she designs as trend-forward embedded with Southern hospitality. Her portfolio boasts spaces that are both sultry and warm, wrapped in Southern charm.

Let's talk about color. How does it impact a space?

Color is such an important and foundational tool for us as we begin to design a space. Once we nail down the vibe the client is going for, reference any historical and geographical parameters that are integral to the design, and build out the layers of a room, the path forward for the color story becomes clearer. For example, if we are designing a gentlemen's lounge we might wrap the room in a rich, dark charcoal gray because it enhances and supports the visual story we want to tell. It also creates the right atmosphere for the people who will experience that room in real life.

What about texture?

Texture is how we push forward or pull back certain colors in a space. If a room is designed around a monochromatic or neutral color scheme, we vary and layer the textures throughout the room to keep that space dynamic and interesting. Texture also plays an important role in the sensory experience of the inhabitant. A part of our process with our clients is to ask questions about the textures they love versus the ones that they hate. This is also particularly important when designing spaces with children who have special needs.

How can functionality impact a space?

One of the foundational philosophies of design is that "form always follows function." This means that the solutions provided for a space should first meet the functional needs of the inhabitants of the space. Then you can jazz up the function by adding form (profiles, fabrics, colors, textures) to enhance the design. Spend some time thinking about what activities you'll be doing in the room and what furnishings you'll need to be able to really use the square footage to its maximum potential. Then draw a rough sketch of your floor plan and furniture arrangement. Play with a few different configurations before you land on the one that feels right to you. Doing this BEFORE you order your new furniture will go a long way toward ensuring that you don't waste money on the wrong pieces!

Arianne Bellizaire pictured in Baton Rouge, Louisiana.

"I love to use limewash and Venetian plaster on the walls. The finishes have a handmade quality to them and a depth that immediately transports you to the Mediterranean."

Faith Blakeney

Many years before Faith Blakeney was an interior designer, she and her sister, Justina (see pages 26–35), owned an eco-fashion company called Compai. While Faith loved all things fashion and creativity, she longed to have a career in interior design—and in her words, she got into the profession "through the back door" as one path serendipitously led to the other.

Faith says, "When I decided to finally heed my heart's desire and transition into interior design, I had a million excuses why I couldn't; I didn't have the right degree, I didn't have a website, I didn't have . . . fill in the blank! I had a realization one night: What is stopping me from living my passion is one thing—myself (and all of these excuses). The very next day I was at a wedding and got approached by one of the guests. She complimented me on the dress I was wearing and asked what I do for work. I took a deep breath and said, 'I'm an interior designer.' She became my first client and through that job I got my next three jobs, and here I am fifteen years later doing what I love every day."

With each room Faith designs, a clear theme runs through: color. She feels that it's the easiest way to change a room. "*Color is everything,*" Faith says. "Color has the power to completely transform a space, and color also has the power to completely change our mood. So choose your colors wisely—color can be our therapy."

How does being a Black designer influence your work?

I come from a very eclectic background. Our papa is Afro-American and Native American and mama is an American-born Russian Jew. We were raised in Berkeley, California, in a home with Barbara Streisand and Sam Cooke always playing in the background. This funky, fantastic mix has brought a richness of culture and spirit to my life, and I believe my designs are an expression of that in many ways. We have a special power as designers to heal, inspire,

OPPOSITE TOP: A bohemian-and-Mediterranean inspired condo Faith Blakeney and her sister Justina designed for their parents. The Hopi Indian photographs were an auction find Faith discovered over two decades ago. OPPOSITE BOTTOM: Recover Integrity, an addiction treatment center operated by Faith's brother in a 7,000-square-foot Mediterranean home in Brentwood, California.

and create understanding and joy through design. As a designer of color, I feel a special calling to create spaces that are a holistic expression of the people who inhabit them—in all of our fantastic funkiness!

What's your go-to design trick?

Fabric! I have an arsenal of fabrics in many different colors and patterns, gathered over the years. I use them to drape over sofas and chairs and side tables, and even hang them on curtain rings with clips for easy-to-change window treatments. Depending on what season it is, or what mood we're in, we can change up our space with fabric. It's mind-blowing how your living room sofa, with a few kantha blankets, mud cloths, or Peruvian frazadas can become a whole new room!

What about texture?

Texture is such a subtle and profound element in design. I love to use limewash and specialty finishes like Venetian plaster on the walls to imbue spaces with texture and life. The finishes have a handmade quality to them and a depth that immediately transports you to the Mediterranean.

How do you bring in the outdoors with your designs?

I use plants, plants, plants. I also bring in colors from nature (greens, rust tones, blues) and natural materials (wood, stone, jute, grasscloth, metal) to create a dialogue between the indoors and outdoors. Funny enough, when designing outdoor spaces I also like to bring the indoors outside. In a place like Los Angeles, California, where I live and work, the weather is so great year-round that we like to take advantage and treat our outdoor spaces with as much care and love as the indoor ones. We bring lighting, rugs, and comfortable furniture outside to create very livable spaces in the great outdoors.

How do you get to know clients and their lives to design their space?

Growing up with parents who are doctors in psychology, we were raised with a curiosity for humans and human nature. When I meet a new client, I take a deep dive because I want their home to represent them. I want to understand not only what their "style" is, and their favorite colors, I want to know where they are at in life, who they are, and who they want to be. Our spaces represent us, and our spaces can call us into being or drag us down. I aim to create spaces that make my clients' hearts sing, and to do that I need to understand the beat of their drum.

Does scale play a factor in your designs?

Scale always plays a big role in the design process. Frank Lloyd Wright was known to build small doorways so that when he stood in the doorway—at a mighty 5′7″—he looked and felt tall! This is a game of scale and proportion, and when you know how to play that game it's an incredible tool for the tool kit.

Do you have a design philosophy or something that you go by as a designer?

Good design comes from a sacred combination of true self-expression, honoring Mother Nature and human nature, and trusting your intuition. I am also a strong believer that good vibes during the design process are an essential ingredient to good results.

What do you want people to remember about you?

I believe that each and everyone of us has gifts, unique talents, and perspectives to bring to the table. I want to be remembered as someone who used my gifts to not only create beauty, but to elevate spirits and create a positive, sustainable impact on our planet, and inspire others to do the same.

A modern eclectic powder room with an upcycled vintage dresser as the vanity. The limewash on the walls was a custom finish created by Faith Blakeney.

"Homing in on your own feelings and how certain colors make you feel is a great jumping-off place for deciding a color palette for a room."

Justina Blakeney

The path to interior design was indirect for designer, artist, and entrepreneur Justina Blakeney. A love for textiles and prints originally led her to a career in fashion, where she spent several years before making the ultimate decision to follow her heart and start her internationally known design and home decor brand, Jungalow.

Someone whose work conjures imagery of plentiful plants and bold colors and patterns, Justina eschews traditional design rules for the most part, focusing more on flow and on the vibe a space brings. Through her roots and approach, Justina reimagines interior spaces as well as the experience someone has in their home.

"Design in the home should be about supporting well-being," she says. "When we think about art and design, we think about what it looks like. I really try to make it about what it feels like—that kind of visceral response that people have to a space, where you walk in somewhere and are in awe and you're looking around with that feeling of, 'Wow, I am surrounded by beauty,' or wonder or surprise or calm. Those are the kinds of things I try to elicit from the spaces that I design. It might not be all about how it looks."

Justina, above all, encourages others to notice what lights them up, or gives them good feelings, and to put those things in their space. "For me, it's about the experience in the room itself and how it makes us feel throughout the day and how it supports us." She adds, "Your home can support your dreams."

How did you get into design?

I've always been a creative person and I've always known I wanted to work in a creative field, but I never really knew exactly how that would manifest. If I were to drill down to what made me want to get into design in the first place, my sister Faith (see pages 22–25), who's a few years older than me, was always

Mixing bold colors, effervescent patterns, and organic materials like wood, plants, and terra cotta is a signature pillar of Justina Blakeney's design ethos.

"I'll keep tweaking until I take a step back and I look at it and then I get that little tingling feeling in my core and then I know, okay, yes, this place has all the feels. This is what we want. We're here. We've arrived."

really interested in interior design. After a number of years working in the fashion industry, I slowly started to get more and more interested in the home space, and I felt like a lot of the things that I loved about fashion design also translated to home.

How does being a Black designer influence your work?

I draw so much on who I am and my personal identity and my heritage in my design work. Jungalow is an expression of who I am and all the different parts of me and my roots. Inevitably my cultural heritage comes out in my design work. Being a designer of color, being a designer with an African heritage, is something that I'm really proud of and something that I think people can sense and feel in my design work.

What about color?

I love color and I think part of my secret to success has been embracing color. When I'm designing for myself or if I'm designing something for a client, I really like to understand not just what their favorite color is, but how different colors make them feel.

So, for example, in my current home, I really wanted to add a feeling of warmth to our living room, which has very high ceilings. I thought to myself, *What's the feeling I want to have in here? I want a feeling of warmth and something that feels inviting and cozy.* So we ended up painting the walls in two tones; in a terra-cotta and in a very light pink to add that warmth. And now, as soon as people walk into the home, they'll say, "Your home is so warm and inviting."

Thinking about how you want to feel in the different areas of your home can very much inform what colors you end up choosing for the walls. Once I understand the overall color palette of the walls, then that's when I get into the color pairings.

And so, I say, "Oh, the way that plants look in front of terra-cotta walls really lights me up." So my accent color for this room is going to be green. Focusing on our own feelings and how certain colors make you feel is a great jumping-off place for deciding a color palette for a room.

Why is it important to layer a room with design elements?

I'm sort of anti-rules when it comes to design. I think of design much more as an art form. Obviously, following rules when it comes to interior architecture and construction and those sorts of things are very important, but when it comes to the final layer, when you're talking about the furnishings and the decor elements to add, I'm not a huge fan of following these very rigid design rules, because every space is different. Every family is different and everyone is going to thrive in a different type of environment.

This sultry living room is a celebration of tone-on-tone color with Farrow & Ball Ointment Pink on the fireplace, Farrow & Ball Breakfast Room Green in the shelves, and Farrow & Ball Pink Ground on the ceiling and upper walls. The tassel pillow is a Loloi Rugs collaboration with Justina Blakeney and takes the 1980s ModernHaus swivel chair to a new graphic level.

Oftentimes photographing a space from different angles can help me see it differently. And then what I say to myself is, "Is this space giving me all the feels?" If it's not giving me all the feels, chances are one of those things is off. Maybe the scale is off, maybe the texture is off, maybe the colors are off, and then I'll keep tweaking until I take a step back and I look at it and then I get that little tingling feeling in my core and then I know, okay, yes, this place has all the feels. This is what we want. We're here. We've arrived.

What's your go-to design trick?

It's super important to have an open mind and to try different things out. One of the things that I will often do, especially before I buy anything, is tape things out on the floor to really be able to understand the scale of something and move it around a bunch, even in my mind. Don't just put a sofa where you automatically assume the sofa should go in the room. Keep an open mind and just experiment with furniture.

For example, there might be an area of your home where it feels somewhat empty, but maybe that's the area where you like to do your workouts, or stretch, or have dance parties. Maybe having some amount of open space with no furniture there might feel awkward in some regard, but it's supporting the lifestyle that you want to have. Have fun, experiment, try things out that you wouldn't necessarily think about, tape lots of shapes on the ground to see and be able to help imagine where things would go.

How do you bring in the outdoors with your designs?

I bring the outdoors in through color. I can use inspiration from nature. I use green a lot in design and decor because I love the way I feel when I'm surrounded by green in a forest or on a hike or in a jungle.

Also, I symbolically use things like jungle-licious wallpapers, art that displays wildlife, or leaves and flowers. I also have a thing for house plants. I truly believe that living in a community with nature is healthy and good for mental health.

What do you want people to remember about you?

That I believe that everyone is creative and that everyone has the power to create beauty in the world. I think we're all born with an incredible amount of potential for creativity and it's really about tapping into it and bringing it out and giving yourself the space to explore that creativity.

OPPOSITE TOP LEFT: The Phoenix wallpaper and Mermaid line art are by Justina Blakeney for Jungalow. The bone inlay–striped mirror is from Etsy. The Artifacts Faucet in vibrant brushed bronze and the Spun Glass Translucent Dew Vessel bathroom sink are from Kohler. The vintage wall sconce from Chairish adds a final layer of texture to the vibrant powder room. OPPOSITE TOP RIGHT: 1980s console from Chairish; Moroccan brass mirrors. The carved stool is an early twentieth-century Ethiopian Jimma stool. OPPOSITE BOTTOM LEFT: This Moroccan-inspired kitchen is found in Jungalow headquarters. Paint, El Coyoté limewash from Portola Paints; 8 x 8-inch Alhambra handmade cement tile on backsplash; vintage runner; Diaz rolling kitchen cart by Mistana. OPPOSITE BOTTOM RIGHT: Vintage chairs reupholstered in Justina Blakeney's Tigress fabric, available at Jungalow.

Limewashed walls in Blue Reef from Sydney Harbor Paint Company form a deep and moody backdrop for rattan nightstands by Bielecky Brothers, a 1970s headboard from 1stDibs, and a rug from Justina Blakeney's Jamila Collection with Loloi Rugs.

"Scents for the home don't have to be heavy or perfumy. Scents have the power to alter moods, be calming, reduce stress, and make a space memorable.

Christopher Charles

Being of service is not unfamiliar to Christopher Charles. Pulling influence from Africa and the vibrant colors and textures evocative of that continent, Christopher loves identifying intimate facets of his clients' personalities and translating them into rooms that echo their passions and lifestyles. Though he grew up appreciating interior design and beautiful, functional spaces, not seeing anyone who looked like him working in interior design (which was more common back when he was a youth) meant it was not the first career choice for Christopher. Before becoming a designer, he served the United States for six years in Iraq during Operation Desert Storm and later worked in performance management for a major oil and gas company.

It wasn't until 2015, when Christopher attended a Black Interior Designers Conference and met Kimberly Ward, that he decided to finally launch his own design firm. What had begun as a hobby for Christopher became a full-time passion and sustainable career for the self-taught designer.

For many, the love of design is what drives them—but for Christopher it is so much more. "The process of blending individual pieces to produce a beautiful, livable space is such an amazing experience," Christopher says. He has a strong appreciation for artisans, so the spaces he designs are a curated blend of modern African and Asian influences. His aim, always, is to create luxurious and livable interiors.

"What I love most about interior design is the process of creating something that nobody has seen before, or putting a new twist on something that people have seen before," he notes. "I think about interior design the way I imagine musicians think about music: just to grab inspiration out of the air, get it on paper, and then produce a melody. Instead of writing songs, interior designers create a beautiful picture that people get to live in."

The inspiration for this space was the vibrancy of New Orleans, a style Christopher Charles termed "Festive Luxe." The one-of-a-kind 8 x 10-foot hand-knotted rug was made in Nepal by Tibetans and sourced through Oriental Rug Gallery of Texas, Houston. The art displayed in the space includes, from right to left: *The Gatekeepers*, by Tanya Doskova; *Secrets*, by John Whaley Jr.; and *Untitled* by Santiago Hermes.

"We have always been trailblazers at our core. We are art, we are music, we are everything created in this world. There is nothing too hard for me to handle, based on what my ancestors have gone through."

How does being a Black designer influence your work?

We have always been trailblazers at our core. We are art, we are music, we are everything created in this world. So, when I approach a project, I approach it from a stance that there is nothing too hard for me to handle, based on what my ancestors have gone through. Being comfortable in that creativity is something that I am still growing into, but I would not trade the African American viewpoint that I bring to design for anything in the world. It has allowed me to make some beautiful, creative design choices that would not have been available to me if I were not African American.

Let's talk about color. How does it impact a space?

Color in interior design has the power not only to transform spaces, but it also can change people's moods, the energy in a space, individual mindsets, and their outlook on life. Color is one of the most influential and transformative elements in interior design, and tint, tone, and shade all play a vital role. These three elements allow the precise customization of any color imaginable. Many homeowners are apprehensive about showcasing color in their space for fear of getting it wrong. That's why I think paint samples are a homeowner's best friend. Paint samples allow you to experience colors before making a full-on commitment.

Why is it important to layer a room design?

I love to layer a space, not only with color and textiles, but with varied design styles, decor from around the world, and art. Layering an interior is the same as exhibiting the varied facets of your personality. I encourage clients to incorporate belongings that they love: There is always a way to tie in things that you love into your space, even if that means rotating items seasonally. Another important layer homeowners often overlook is scent. How a space smells is just as important as how it looks and feels. Scents for the home don't have to be heavy or perfumy. Scents have the power to alter moods, be calming, reduce stress, and make a space memorable.

What's your go-to design trick?

I always try to keep the heaviest pieces of furniture up off the floor with a visual trick: placing dark furniture against lighter colored flooring or rugs.

How do you bring in the outdoors with your designs?

My two favorite options are greenery, either natural or high-quality faux plants that provide a real touch experience, and using rustic oversized outdoor pottery inside the home. Showcasing large-leaf greenery is an excellent way to bring the beauty and warmth of the outdoors inside. Using oversized rustic and patinaed pottery as end tables or accent tables also creates a sense of the outdoors—and adds a stylish layer to the design.

What do you want people to remember about you?

I want them to know that I poured every ounce of my humanity into every space that I created. These spaces represent the best of who I am and the greatest hope of my ancestors.

This media space's intended use was a formal dining room. A handmade Brazilian monkey-comb wreath is displayed on the cocktail table. These wreaths are made of locally harvested Brazilian monkey-comb seeds.

A lively and vibrant living room inspired by the client's mother. The heirloom black-and-gold antique hand-painted French papier mâché tea table adds a layer of warmth to the soft dove walls and furniture.

"If a space has a colorful palette, a great way to create contrast is to anchor it with some black."

Nikki Chu

When Nikki Chu uses color in her design projects, it's often through artwork—which is an element in design she thinks should never be an afterthought. "We have more walls than space on the floor," Nikki points out. "Because of this, I believe that, next to lighting, filling the walls with art is what creates a designer-looking space. The scale of the art you choose, the style of the frame, and incorporating art lights above it can elevate your art collection."

Nikki seeks to create rooms with a luxe aesthetic and neutral color palette, bringing in bold pops of color through statement artwork that tells a story. She has a solution for achieving the same look if large artwork is out of the budget: "If you can't afford large-scale prints and art, gallery walls of smaller artworks are a great option as a backdrop to an oversized sofa."

Do you have a design philosophy you go by?
My design philosophy is to create livable spaces that are comfortable, stylish, and glamorous. I love mixing modern and ethnic patterns to create a sophisticated, global, glam look.

Do you have any tips on lighting?
I love lighting; I call it the jewelry of a home. Unfortunately, most people don't hang lights at the appropriate height, which causes a space to look unbalanced. One thing to remember is that a beautiful chandelier over a dining table should hang 64 to 65 inches from the floor to the bottom of the fixture.

What about contrast?
Contrast can be done in many ways, but I love to create contrast with color. If a space has a colorful palette, a great way to create contrast is to anchor it with some black accessories, art, furnishings, or light fixtures.

How do you advise someone to mix patterns in a room?
When designing and using multiple patterns in one space, it is important that you have some sort of through line in the patterns. Typically, I use color as my through line. A simple pattern-mixing concept to ensure balance would look like this: stripes, florals, a small print, a solid texture, a large-scale pattern. If they all have a through line of color, it will allow these to work well together in one space.

How do you think of functionality?
Functionality is really all about how you live. When you first walk through the door, where do you put your keys, your bag, or the mail? I like to walk through a space and imagine how a person lives, where they would need a charging station, or where they would hang a kid's backpack at the front door. All these considerations create the perfect functionality in a space.

What about movement?
Movement can be created by art, textiles, lighting, or drapery. By playing with the weight of fabrics, and with dimmable lights, you can achieve movement in a space.

Designer Nikki Chu posing in Lala Anthony's Brooklyn, New York, home. Nikki used art to minimize the stairwell's presence in the space. The photograph is by Drew Doggett and the black-and-white painting is from Z Gallerie.

"There is nothing I like more than supporting Black artists and having their work in my spaces. And everyone's lives and homes are definitely improved with some funk."

Danielle Colding

Danielle Colding arrived at the career of interior design when she realized she wanted work that proved itself to be different from one day to the next, a constant stream of creativity and problem-solving that provided moments of beauty. She won HGTV's *Design Star* competition in 2012, sending her on a whirlwind experience through her design journey, helping her refine and embolden her style along the way. Now she works with clients to help them create homes that are elegant and comfortable at the same time. "I am all for elegance and ingenuity as long as it is also comfortable," she says. "I never want to be in a space that feels stuffy or overdone. The most lush rooms also need to be approachable."

To achieve this balance, Danielle layers, mixes, and blends elements in a room to make the space feel like it has thoughtfully grown with the homeowner over time.

"Start with the classics, add something old, and make sure there is something a little off and funky in the space," she notes. "Vintage and antique pieces add that certain something that gives rooms their depth. Mixing elements gives spaces a feeling of richness, provenance, and personality. And don't forget dynamic art!"

How did you get into design?

Prior to design I was a modern dancer, schoolteacher, Pilates instructor, and waitress. After a few years, I was burnt out—to say the least. Facing the need to figure something out, I decided to travel. I reflected on what I was naturally good at, what I would enjoy, and what would be different enough on a daily basis to hold my interest. I also thought about how much my mother and I had enjoyed working on my childhood home for my whole life. That's when I arrived at the profession of interior design.

How does being a Black designer influence your work?

Being a Black woman is at the heart of all I do. It is the center of my being and informs all aspects of my work. Black folks in America are always putting a spin on the classics. We are the ultimate innovators. I think of my role here as developing an aesthetic that speaks to a global perspective, giving voice to all different preferences and world views. Perhaps the biggest influence on my work is my choice of artwork. There is nothing I like more than supporting Black artists and having their work in my spaces. And everyone's lives and homes are definitely improved with some funk.

Let's talk about color. How does it impact a space?

Color is everything and is usually where I start my creative process. I push myself to come up with innovative combinations that sing in some unique way. There is a real magic to finding a balance that feels good and still pushes the creative envelope. The crucial part about color is not to match too perfectly. Having a slightly off color gives a room visual interest and depth.

Danielle Colding photographed in her own prewar Upper West Side apartment. It is located in the Shangri-La area of New York City and combines carefully chosen textures throughout.

44

"The crucial part about color is not to match too perfectly. I have definitely learned that lesson the hard way. Having a slightly off color gives a room visual interest and depth."

Why is it important to layer a room?

Design is all about layering. Starting with a good foundation is key, and building from there is the great work we get to do. I usually start with the color, wall finishes, and large furniture pieces. From there the smaller one-off items, lighting, window treatments, accessories, and art go in. One perfectly placed object can absolutely transform a space. It is the final layered elements that bring the heart and soul into a room.

What about focal points?

Focal points 100 percent depend on the space itself. As a designer you have to honor the architecture. So sometimes one focal point makes sense. Sometimes you want to create an enveloping space where your eye can dance around to a number of different directions.

Do you have a design philosophy or something that you go by as a designer?

My philosophy is all about making a space that reflects who my clients are, meeting their functional needs, and pushing the envelope in terms of creativity. I am all for elegance and ingenuity as long as it is also comfortable. I never want to be in a space that feels stuffy or overdone. The most lush rooms also need to be approachable or else, in my book, it's a fail. And I always, always, always focus on artwork!

What do you want people to remember about you?

I want people to remember my versatility. I'd like people to see that my work is not formulaic. That I made choices and designed in the moment, for that client in a way that worked with the unique space. I really like all different styles and I like that my work reflects that. Don't put this baby in the corner!

OPPOSITE TOP LEFT: The leisure area with a plush patterned rug from ABC Carpet & Home, a Vladimir Kagan Nautilus chair, and Pierre Malbec painting from Balsamo Antiques. OPPOSITE TOP RIGHT: Upper West Side dining room with vintage wooden side chairs and mid-century modern upholstered header chairs. OPPOSITE BOTTOM LEFT: Vignette featuring artwork by Jerome Lagarrigue. OPPOSITE BOTTOM RIGHT: Custom upholstered bed from Design Within Reach, pendant light from Lumfardo Luminaires, and artwork by Jerome Lagarrigue.

"Soft, luxurious fabrics like velvet, mohair, and cashmere can be set against concrete or wood to bring balance and warmth. Plus, they are fun to touch."

Bridgid Coulter Cheadle

Bridgid Coulter Cheadle was raised in Berkeley, California, and credits both her heritage and the city of her upbringing with the style and mindset she brings into each design project. "I'm grateful to live my life through the lens of Blackness both personally and as a designer," Bridgid says. "Growing up Black in America and the very quirky nature of a multicultural city like Berkeley permeate my way of thinking. There is an experimental attitude toward education, work, and human interaction that has made me who I am as a designer, entrepreneur, and philanthropist overall. Outside the box is my inside the box. My work is informed by society, culture, and community. I always infuse that sensibility into my work and am inspired to infuse the heritage of my clients into their spaces as well."

From the start of any project, Bridgid finds inspiration from the clients' heritage, thoughtfully selecting pieces that feature the beauty that is found in their lineage. "Carefully placed items, fixtures, fittings, and surface materials can add to the visual interest and create an energy that infuses a room with style," she notes.

Some of these items can even serve as a room's focal points, in Bridgid's opinion. "Focal points really come into play when you have something special you want to feature—a chandelier, a sculpture, a vintage or antique chair, or a family heirloom. A home can have a wow moment or two that stand out; but then the rest of the space can have a series of design vignettes, which I like to think of as the ensemble or support players in a play."

Putting compelling sentimental items in the starring role of the room will set the tone of the space to show a uniqueness that is only found in each individual person and family, Bridgid says. "If our homes and living spaces are essentially a container for our personal stories, then these moments offer an opportunity to explore and experience the story of the inhabitants of the space—their culture, history, accomplishments, and even aspirations."

The refectory dining room table in this Venice, California, great room was repurposed from another project and is flanked by Emeco 111 Navy Chairs made from recycled plastic bottles. Bridgid Coulter Cheadle completed the space with French oak floors and vintage rugs.

This outdoor living area in a 1920s Spanish Colonial Revival home located in Brentwood, California, features a custom Moroccan coffee table designed by Bridgid Coulter Cheadle.

55

"I place the largest sofa or sectional possible in a room to ground the space (short of blocking walkways, obviously). I find it makes the space feel more expansive and larger."

How did you get into design?

In retrospect, I realize that my beloved grandmother was one of the original influencers leading to my future design acumen. We grew up across the street from my grandparents in Berkeley, California, and their home provided the heart to all family gatherings. Holidays were big deals. My grandmother was always a stylish woman, but she also managed to design a house filled with love, laughter, and beauty. The walls were bright, happy hues of cream and marigold with intriguing local art and photography that never lost its interest. The carpet complemented it very well and served as a solid base to comfortable, well-placed key furniture pieces that invited family conversation.

How does texture impact a space?

Texture is one of those elements that adds to the sensory delight of a space. Soft, luxurious fabrics like velvet, mohair, and cashmere can be set against concrete or wood to bring balance and warmth. Plus, they are fun to touch. A successful layering of texture also adds to the overall visual enjoyment of a space and can indicate whether there's an expectation of seriousness or play.

How do you bring in the outdoors with your designs?

Pattern is one of my favorite ways to bring the outdoors in with design. You can bring in textiles with large graphics such as florals and monstera leaves, or grasscloth wallpaper painted with ombré effects that echo the sky at sunset.

How important is scale?

Scale is essential to every design. Selecting items, surface materials, fixtures, and fittings that are the right size for your space can make all the difference. It may be counterintuitive, but placing something that is actually too small for a space can make the space feel smaller and off balance. This has especially been my experience with sofas—wherever possible I place the largest sofa or sectional possible in a room to ground the space (short of blocking walkways, obviously). I find it makes the space feel more expansive and larger.

OPPOSITE TOP: A transitional open kitchen in Kona, Hawaii. Dark-stained oak cabinetry, solid surface countertops, and a Carrara marble backsplash create a monochromatic palette that brings warmth and contrast and opens to the outdoors. There is a double island/bar. The flow of food preparation and entertainment give an added layer of functionality for the space. OPPOSITE BOTTOM: A tranquil bedroom suite with layers of texture including soft graphic wallpaper, graphic window treatments, and organic accents.

"Visit showrooms to sit on seating, or even try boxing out rooms with tape on the floor of an intended space to give you a better sense of size and scale."

Adair Curtis

Adair Curtis has loved design for as long as he can remember. As a child, he would dream while flipping through the pages of shelter magazines and then apply his findings to rooms in his family home. Now he designs homes for a living through the multidisciplinary studio he shares with his husband, stylist Jason Bolden.

With a style that blends laid-back luxury with organic sensibilities, Adair reminds us that a balanced space isn't always about symmetry. "Balance refers to the artful distribution of visual weight in a space, with symmetry being the most time-honored and easiest way to achieve balance in a space," he begins, "but asymmetrical pieces of similar weight can also be a way to achieve balance. It's in the asymmetrical that we thrive! One tip I like to suggest to achieve balance that may not be that obvious is incorporating negative space. Sometimes, all a space needs is nothing. This allows for the pieces and objects to breathe."

Using negative space thoughtfully is a smart tool that Adair uses, but he also suggests using art when it comes to puzzling walls or spaces. "Art has the ability to be a subtle accessory in a space, or a highlighted focal point," he says. "No matter the purpose, adding art to a space is a beautiful way to express oneself. One trick I lean in to is using art on awkward walls and spaces. It's a way to give these peculiar spots purpose."

Why is it important to layer a room with design elements?
Even the staunchest minimalists know layering is key to a room feeling complete. There's a saying that goes, "The eye has to travel." In this case, layering gives the eye oftentimes unique and interesting things to land on, which ultimately makes rooms feel finished.

How do you bring in the outdoors with your designs?
Some of the ways in which we bring the outdoors into our designs is by incorporating elements indoors that you naturally find outdoors. For rooms with high ceilings, we incorporate tall potted trees, at times build textured living walls of moss and other greenery, highlight outdoor gardens through strategically planned windows, and, in some cases where possible, remove ceilings or install retractable roofs to truly allow the outdoors in. We carry design elements from indoors to the outdoors as well.

Do you have a design philosophy or something that you go by as a designer?
For our residential clients, we believe homes should be a reflection of the people who occupy them. With that said, our approach is to help clients discover what motivates them, what excites them, what inspires them, what they find beautiful, and to have that be reflected in our projects.

Adair Curtis (left) is pictured with his husband, stylist Jason Bolden (right). The featured background art is by Mattea Perrotta. On the table, the painting of the boy in the yellow sweater is by Gerald Lovell, and the photo of the giraffes is by Peter Beard. The lamp is by Paavo Tynell.

How does being a Black designer influence your work?

I am the cumulation of all of my experiences. Black people and experiences aren't monolithic, but, depending on where you're from, the chances are high that you'll have a ton of shared experiences with your peers. I bring all of those experiences and perspectives to all I do in design. That will look different from project to project, but I view my being Black as a creative advantage—one of my superpowers, if you will.

How can lighting impact a space?

Lighting is a crucial element to any great design. Great lighting and the fixtures it comes from help to set the tone and the illusion of space of a room. Always ensure there are a variety of lighting sources, and at multiple levels, throughout a space. Another great tip I find is to incorporate your lighting on dimmers wherever possible.

How do you use contrast in your designs?

Contrast in design is all about using tension to articulate and illustrate a point. It's big vs. small, light vs. dark, bright vs. dull, and masculine vs. feminine, to name a few. We use these opposing points in most of our projects. For example, we use both contemporary and antique pieces for many of our modern projects. This juxtaposition tends to add warmth and soul to spaces that usually feel void and empty.

How do you incorporate functionality in your designs?

Interior design is not all about aesthetics. What good is a space that doesn't have functionality at its core for the end user? For this reason, functionality and aesthetics go hand in hand. We do this by ensuring that not only does the furniture we choose for a space fit and look good, but that everything works for the people that live within a space. For example, a number of our clients are professional athletes, and they are much taller than the average person. For these clients, we explore seating heights and depths to allow for their maximum comfort. The best way to know if something will work for a design functionality-wise is to try things out. Visit showrooms to sit on seating, or even try boxing out rooms with tape on the floor of an intended space to give you a better sense of size and scale.

What do you want people to remember about you?

While I'd love for people to remember particular things about my design aesthetic and approach, I'd be most honored if the people I've worked with or had the pleasure to come across remembered me for how I made them feel and what value I added to their lives in whatever small way that may be.

OPPOSITE TOP: An oversized Croft House sofa and a Marcel Breuer vintage chair shape the monochromatic living room, while the custom Carrara marble plinth coffee table adds a smooth layer of texture. OPPOSITE BOTTOM: This Beverly Hills bedroom includes a velvet gray chair and bed from B&B Italia and a custom bronze mirror.

"The rhythm in a space is akin to a musical beat—what flows for one person may not flow for the other. Design is personal and so is our space."

Brenda Danso

Brenda Danso describes the act of designing a room very much like painting on a blank canvas or weaving a traditional kente cloth. Her use of color and impact in her designs often fuses modern spaces with clean lines, striking imagery, and patterns to result in visual harmony.

"Color has the ability to elicit emotion, so when done strategically color has the power to uplift and elicit joy," she says. This understanding and embrace of vibrant color, on Brenda's part, has much to do with her heritage and home country of Ghana.

"I was born in Ghana—I come from a very rich culture," she says. "Ghana is colorful in so many ways; the people are vibrant, the food is flavorful, and the textiles are brightly colored. Ghana is known for the kente fabric, a cloth that is uniquely handwoven. Each design symbolizes meaning and tells a story. Similarly, my design often incorporates use of color and is inspired by the client's experience. Each project holds an important story with meaning. As Black designers, there is a unique experience that we bring to the design industry; we view art and design from a unique lens based on our diverse history."

How did you get into design?

The real estate market was booming in Toronto in 2017. I became intrigued with the art of staging homes, and I started working with local real estate agents to transform properties that were being listed for sale. As I embarked on this new journey, I received an overwhelming response from homeowners who wanted to redesign their space after seeing my staging work. This propelled my transition into design.

This worldly and refreshing office was designed by Brenda Danso with healing in mind. The Benny Bing art establishes a subtle focal point in the room.

A soft and elegant girls' bedroom combines traditional bed frames with striking modern wallpaper.

How do you bring in the outdoors with your designs?

I am always inclined to add texture through natural elements, whether it is a swing made with natural wood, or a side table made from a tree stump. Even the simplicity of a window view can inspire you to bring in branches and add them to a vase or pick pampas grass to add to your decor.

How do you get to know clients and their lives to design their space?

At the moment that I step into a client's space, I have little interest in the design. My goal is to learn as much about my clients as possible. My best interactions with them take place at the dining table over tea while exchanging stories. The experience stays with me, and that is what informs the design. At this point, I know what drives the client and what inspires them. Once this is captured, the design becomes personal and, most importantly, meaningful.

Does scale play a factor in your designs?

Although scale is important in a space, the best indicator of how one object relates to another is personal. So overall, a good designer will ensure that things are proportioned and not out of place; however, the rhythm in the space can help create the balance that is needed. The rhythm in a space is akin to a musical beat—what flows for one person may not flow for the other. Design is personal and so is our space.

What about focal points?

A focal point is very important when designing a space. Imagine walking into a space and your eyes are drawn to a focal wall with intriguing art, or intricate flooring that guides your journey. Focal points can be used strategically to guide one into a space. When I think about my favorite restaurants, they are often spaces that use various focal points to create an experience. Those spaces are memorable and embedded in my memory. They're places I want to continue to experience. A focal point can leave a lasting impression.

Do you have a design philosophy or something that you go by as a designer?

Design is flexible and rules can be broken; creating a space that elicits emotions and has meaning and purpose is of priority. This kind of space will always draw a deeper connection.

What do you want people to remember about you?

I want people to remember the impact I have made on their life. I strongly believe that design is therapeutic—it has the ability to heal, the ability to help problem solve. I want to continue to interact and engage with people in a way that feels impactful, whereby designing a space becomes the bonus.

OPPOSITE TOP LEFT: Home office details featuring art by Sarah Rutledge. OPPOSITE TOP RIGHT: The living room features monochromatic texture. OPPOSITE BOTTOM LEFT: A detail from the dining room. OPPOSITE BOTTOM RIGHT: Modern powder room with a bold printed wallpaper from THE GOODS by shay and a textured vanity from 3D VR Designs.

"The best spaces are collected, so I always encourage my clients to be open and give their design room to grow as they continue to experience life and live in their space."

Anthony Dunning

Anthony Dunning has spent plenty of time thinking about the stories a space can tell through decor and design. He owned a furniture consignment store in his hometown and constantly saw storied pieces come and go. This ever-changing flow of different furniture and pieces translates into his design work, where he truly believes that you must leave room for discovery throughout the design process and decorating your home.

"My design philosophy is to give your design room to grow," Anthony says. "Even as a designer I am constantly sharpening my skills with each new space and opportunity. It's important to understand that a design is never truly done. As we continue to live and have different experiences, our needs change, and we should continue to improve our homes. Understanding this relieves us of the stress of feeling like we have to have all of the answers right now."

While allowing flexibility for life, Anthony offers some foundational tips for creating movement and a cohesive impact on a room at the same time. "Movement affects the flow and rhythm in space. One of the ways I incorporate movement is in repetition. I will often make a room's ceiling and trim the same color as the wall. Also, I like the idea of utilizing uniform materials, especially when it comes to floors and stones throughout a home."

Let's talk about color. How does it impact a space?
Color is impactful when it is utilized within the guidelines of a client's needs and personality. I'm a designer who considers different shades of white as color. Saturated colors are not for everyone, and I've seen everything from deep jewel tones to various whites elevate rooms. It's all about what the person inhabiting the space needs to thrive.

How do you bring in the outdoors with your designs?
One of the first things I do when designing a home or room is identify its exposures. I'm looking for the

Anthony Dunning's Upper West Side residence in New York includes the bold Mr. Fantasy eye print pillow, a custom sofa designed by the designer, and strategically placed vintage pieces from favorite flea markets in Paris and Padua, Italy.

"Making big gestures, even in small spaces, immediately gives a room more importance. Large-scale artwork, coffee tables, sculptures, and light fixtures are a few of the areas where I like to push the limits."

color of reflection the house receives from the exterior surroundings. Houses surrounded by a lot of trees tend to receive a green and/or yellow cast, while apartments in New York City often receive blue or gray tones. Understanding this and incorporating it in your design scheme is paramount in making sure your selections are shown in their best light.

Does scale play a factor in your designs?

Scale plays a major role in my designs, and I'm one to scale up in many cases. Making big gestures, even in small spaces, immediately gives a room more importance. Large-scale artwork, coffee tables, sculptures, and light fixtures are a few of the areas where I like to push the limits.

How can lighting impact a space?

There is no element that is more important in design. It is through lighting that you present and establish the energy of a space. A mixture of ambient, task, and accent lighting is integral and powerful in the grand scheme of design. When it comes to lighting, determine what lighting you need to function and then decide what you would like to highlight.

Traditional dining room with creamy floor-to-ceiling cabinetry, cool tones and warm wooden accents, and oversized windows overflowing with natural light.

What are some tips for using art in a space?

Nothing defines the identity of a room better than art, in my opinion. Art is a great way to tell your story and present those themes and ideas that are important in your life! I combine a mix of paintings, photography, and sculpture in each project to present a well-rounded and curated sensibility.

How can balance impact a room?

Understanding balance can require a bit of trial and error. My greatest advice as it relates to balance is to not be afraid to try things. Sometimes I like to grab a few options and try them, and, as a space reveals itself to me, I become more familiar with what actually works in any given circumstance. Selecting pairs of items and pieces of similar scale and proportion is a great way to bring balance to a room.

How do you incorporate sustainability in your designs?

I always incorporate new and old things in the spaces I design. Something with a bit of history is a great way to ground a space. Even if I'm working on an ultramodern space, I like to slip in an item that tells a story of the space. The best spaces are collected, so I always encourage my clients to be open and give their design room to grow as they continue to experience life and live in their space. Giving new life to furniture from antique shops, consignment shops, and flea markets is a great way to contribute toward sustainability.

How does being a Black designer influence your work?

Being a Black designer has taught me the importance of flexibility, personal vision, and resilience. I know that the business of home has been significantly impacted by the contributions of people who look like me throughout history. Black labor and ingenuity was and is important to the fabric of America and was instrumental in formalizing what it means to establish and develop a home to this day. This legacy sustains me as I navigate the intricacies of creative work and the industry.

What do you want people to remember about you?

I want people to remember that I was passionate and unafraid of taking risks in design. I want to be remembered for dynamic spaces that leave a lasting impression and environments that improve my clients' way of life.

A well-layered bedroom vignette boasts a print by Jessica Strahan, a vintage chair reupholstered in Lee Jofa fabric, and a lamp from Stein World. The space is anchored with a moody wallpaper print from Union Rustic. The upholstered leather door with nailhead trim is custom.

"I believe that color equals joy, color equals love, and color equals soul. I have no desire to live in a black and white world (in any capacity) and seek to infuse color (and fun) in all aspects of my life."

Kelly Finley

Kelly Finley's path to designing through her firm Joy Street Design came to her first as a creative outlet when she was working as a litigation attorney in San Francisco. Her attorney colleagues and friends became her first design clients, and she began her transition from law into interior design. "I'm forever thankful for their support as I honed my new craft," she shares. Kelly moved to Los Angeles, struck out on her own to start her design firm, and hasn't looked back.

How does being a Black designer influence your work?

My design style is simple, modern, and colorful. I love clean lines and simple silhouettes, but I also always need to have something that is very colorful. Joy Street Design is known for its deft use of color. I believe that color equals joy, color equals love, and color equals soul. I have no desire to live in a black and white world (in any capacity) and seek to infuse color (and fun) in all aspects of my life. My cultural background and childhood memories shape my style. As a Black child in Chicago, I grew up in a house full of color, art, and vibrancy. I don't think I had ever been in a room that was all white before moving to college. The idea that color equals joy and happiness was ingrained in me from an early age.

What's your go-to design trick up your sleeve?

I am an expert in space planning and being able to see how a space should be configured immediately. With a background in math and computer science in college, I love interior design because it is mostly about problem solving. There are a variety of answers, but it is a question that allows you to apply your skills and education for a client. And most importantly, you can solve the problem in a creative and gorgeous way. When I walk into any space, I see how it should be laid out almost instinctively—it's the best part of the job for me.

OPPOSITE TOP: Oakland dining room with ombré wallpaper, blue velvet dining chairs, and a carved wooden sideboard for added texture. OPPOSITE BOTTOM: A cozy Oakland breakfast nook painted in Benjamin Moore Ultra Violet. The marble backsplash is from Ann Sacks.

"I think we get hung up a lot on focal points as opposed to telling a story that kind of runs the room and is able to create different vignettes."

Tavia Forbes & Monet Masters

Through bold sophistication and endless personality, Tavia Forbes and Monet Masters work together to dream up spaces that perfectly reflect and inspire the people who live there.

"I think the first thing that we're inspired by is our client, outside of wanting to design something that's bold and memorable and eclectic," Tavia says. "Our clients have a significant influence on what we create, because we want the space to reflect them. It is really challenging, and also fun, to translate a personality into a space—it's what keeps the designs looking different each time."

With their design firm, Forbes Masters, Tavia and Monet take their clients through a very detailed interview process—down to pets, colors, whether they eat in the living room, and so on. This gives them the starting point for each room.

"What I love most is finding the starting point," Monet says. "It's really easy to flow through the design and to have an ending because there [are] so many great options. But to land on where we start, it's fun. Sometimes it is the client's travels, sometimes it is artifacts, sometimes it is a sofa that's been passed down. Or it may be a fabric, a color, or a reference to a trip or a hotel."

Let's talk about color. How does it impact a space?

MONET & TAVIA: Color adds boldness and depth, and it sets a mood. In color theory, color evokes emotion and energy—there's a color for every mood. Technically speaking, we like to utilize that concept, especially for bedrooms, formal dining rooms, and more intimate enclosed spaces.

Why is it important to layer a room design?

TAVIA: Layering a room is the art of interior design: ensuring that there is a focal point; adequate, adjustable lighting; as well as textures that speak to one another, for cohesion and even a little bit of tension. Layering, right down to the accessories, creates the personality of the space. It is key to have the space planning first, then layer in wall details, floor coverings, lighting, upholstery fabrics, and more—all lend to the function of a space and how it's going to feel for the inhabitants.

Do you have a go-to design trick?

TAVIA: [Thinking about how our design affects] all six "walls" or surfaces; the floor, ceiling, and all four walls. I think that's a starting point for us. We always do this exercise: We choose some pretty furniture, then plan the walls—asking ourselves, how are we introducing a new texture, be it wallpaper, paint, window treatment, wood and stone? Since we work a lot in Atlanta (where the architecture can be new and not very interesting), we are always trying to create a fresh environment and to change the space with wall texture.

Can you touch more on texture?

MONET: I think texture just invites the experience through another sense. Typically, we walk in the room for the reveal, and the clients take in a beautiful design visually. Then we invite them to also feel and touch this space. There have been several times when clients were almost afraid to touch the things

LEFT TO RIGHT: Monet Masters and Tavia Forbes, photographed for their wallpaper collection. Statue is from Curated Home Brands.

because because it was all so new and foreign to them and pretty. We've had to usher them in to touch it and sit in it and feel it because it also contributes to the experience of living in that space. That's why texture is important: It intensifies the experience within a space. It's also a tool that can define the design style in each space.

How do you bring the outdoors into your designs?

TAVIA: We are always inspired by nature, whether by colors or textures or certain themes and schemes that we see outdoors. Sometimes it can be spirals or repetition—and many times we get inspiration from nature for color stories and we build upon that.

Is scale a factor in your designs?

TAVIA: Scale plays a role in creating zones and focal points. For small spaces, people naturally lean toward small furniture, thinking that is what will fit. However, you can play with dimension and oversized elements to trick the eye into thinking the room is larger than it really is. There is a fine, fine balance in playing with scale and calling attention to things that we want to beef up versus the other items in the room.

How do you implement focal points in a space? How important are they?

MONET: I think that, kind of piggybacking on the previous question and answer, scale can also play a part in creating a functional, well-designed space and in creating art. Oftentimes now we're seeing a lot more minimal spaces where the designer is being very intentional about nothing being around that bed because there's very large-print wallpaper. Similarly, when it comes to focal point, oftentimes we'll walk into showrooms and we'll see these beautiful vignettes, and there's layers and layers and items on top of items and it's just creating this beautiful look but there is no focal [point] there. It's just like a whole bunch of beautiful things; but I think that when designing for a client and it's typically a high-use space, we don't get the opportunity to design in that way where there's not a focal point. Because these spaces [we design] are functioning spaces, and the interior architecture sometimes lends a hand in showing us where that focal point is going to be in that room.

TAVIA: And to add to that, I think we get hung up a lot on focal points as opposed to telling a story that kind of runs the room and is able to create different vignettes that have a different feel. [For us,] focal points are strong throughout the room and they're telling different stories, because you're not looking at a room from one view or one picture when you're experiencing it. It's 360 degrees.

How does being a Black designer influence your work?

MONET: The number-one way that it influences my work is because I'm still catering to my clients. It influences my work in ways of integrity and ambition. It's not enough to just be creative and be an interior designer and be an artist, because if it were so, I feel like I would be granted or have the

"Texture is important: it intensifies the experience within a space. It's also a tool that can define the design style in each space."

This Ladies Lounge was designed for the 2022 Atlanta Home for the Holidays Showhouse, inspired by the Arte mural *Secret Silhouettes*. Photography by Tokie Rome-Taylor, African bust (made of terra-cotta) by Nhut Nhathawut. Vintage pedestal under the statue. Custom pillows by Aurielle Jones of Stud Pillows.

same ideas or same exposure as a lot of my other colleagues. Being Black makes me work harder. It makes me constantly think about the next move and constantly move forward because, whether we like it or not, we are constantly proving and reiterating our value. You're always fighting for your value.

TAVIA: I guess on the negative side to Monet's last point about continually having to prove yourself and also being undervalued, we sometimes see each other and then others see us and the assumption is that we would provide a discounted service. And while we're providing the same level of service, and providing our creativity and our thoughtfulness, we should have a value on that creativity and on the service provided.

So that's the fight or the struggle with being a Black designer. Especially being a Black female designer. We're at essentially the bottom of the tier for people's perceived value. And I think we're each out here now proving our value as designers every day. It's like everyone kind of looked up and realized, oh, wow, there is something. They exist. And it's like we were completely invisible, because we were invisible outside of our own community. We all knew each other, but the larger community didn't see us, and they see us now. We are now more exposed to other great designers—which is insanely inspiring—who we didn't even see before because they weren't published. But they were out here doing phenomenal work this whole time. Which is beautiful.

This home office in Morningside/Lenox Park, Georgia, mixes function and fun with bold upholstered wallpaper from Arte as a backdrop for the client's podcast. Custom tassel art from Caralarga and a repurposed zebra chair are from the client's previous home.

"I love playing with specialty lighting (such as LED tape lighting) that enhances shelving, walls, and other elements. It will make the space feel more luxe."

Amhad Freeman

When it comes to using color, Amhad Freeman likes to stay away from hues that overexcite the brain. His style is a mix of what he calls "dreamy minimalism," and it results in homes that are neutral in tone and pared back when it comes to decorative items. This approach is intended to let the room help calm the mood of those who inhabit it.

"Colors in the interior definitely influence your mood," he begins. "I stay away from loud colors and colors that stimulate the mind to be active. Instead, I love using colors that are soothing, because I believe the home should be a refuge from the fast pace of day-to-day activities. Neutrals and calming colors are what I enjoy using in the spaces I design."

The same goes for texture and contrast—since he aims to design rooms that feel restful on the brain and mood, he isn't focused on creating moments with bold elements. "The only time I use contrast is with textures," he says. "I try to keep the same color tones and shades in my designs to create a relaxing feel throughout the project."

For anyone looking for a starting place with setting the style or vibe for their space, Amhad suggests turning to your closet or daily activities for the answer. "I often spend time getting to know the client's lifestyle. Most importantly, I pay attention to how the client dresses. It will tell me if they are formal or casual, colorful or neutral, tailored or more relaxed."

How does being a Black designer influence your work?
Being a Black Southerner brings a certain charm to my business operations and design work. I would argue that being Black has made me stand out in a crowd, have a totally different outlook on the homes I design, and be able to spread education to potential clients as well as to potential designers that want to pursue a career in design.

Why is it important to layer a room with design elements?
Layers in a room are paramount! Rooms without layers can come across as flat and boring. Layering a room can be challenging and often confusing, but if you get it right, the room comes to life and becomes exciting. I love to design and decorate with neutrals and monochromatic colors, so I need to play with textures. I often mix hard and soft, light and dark, smooth and rough materials.

What about focal points?
I am not a designer that focuses on focal points or focal walls. The magic of my process is to make the eye dance around the room and not just look at one element.

What's your go-to design trick?
I love playing with specialty lighting (such as LED tape lighting) that enhances shelving, walls, and other elements. This does not have to cost a ton of money, but it will make the space feel more luxe.

Ahmad Freeman, photographed in a Chicago project showcasing the designer's signature minimalist luxe aesthetic.

> *"I recommend using patterns that are more geometrical. This brings more order to the space and design."*

Speaking of, how can lighting impact a space?

Lighting is *everything* and I put it everywhere, as LED tape lighting can be your best friend when designing. My advice would be to invest in a good designer who has an excellent lighting expert in their contacts.

How do you bring in the outdoors with your designs?

I often use outdoor furniture that looks like it should go inside. I use materials that are softer and make sure they are cohesive to the furnishings on the inside of the home.

How do you incorporate patterns in your designs?

Patterns add excitement to a space. I do like to use patterns, but they need to have the same tone and mood as to the rest of the space. I am not one to use lots of bold patterns as I feel it distracts from the flow of the space. I favor geometric patterns because they add visual order.

Do you have a design philosophy or something that you go by as a designer?

Design to your highest ability, but don't overdo it.

OPPOSITE: Conceptual space by the designer featuring bronze trim details on the walls and rug border. The large wooden table is from Davidson London, the textured credenza is from Olivya Stone, and the cool velvet chairs are from Aiveen Daly.
ABOVE: The graceful vintage piano and custom silk window treatments set the tone for this luxurious traditional sitting room.

"I love interesting lamps and mega chandeliers that make a bold statement. You don't need to light the whole room, you can add ambiance to different areas within a room."

Joan Goodwin

Joan Goodwin is one of the original Top 20 African American Interior Designers. Joan specializes in timeless luxury interiors, and shared with *Architectural Digest*, "I feel it is important not to compromise the integrity of the future for present-day design." Through her firm, Verandah Interiors, spaces are heavily influenced by the experiences Joan has encountered through her travels.

How does color impact space?
Colors change our perception of interior spaces. Lighter colors can make interiors feel larger and more spacious, while darker hues can make spaces feel smaller and cozier. I love working with true, vibrant colors that evoke energy or calmness.

Does scale play a factor in your designs?
Scale is always a factor in my design. If the room is small, I consider the pattern. I use smaller prints and fewer of them. A larger room can handle larger prints and more colors. If I am using a large print in a small room, I make sure it has lots of white space in it, and use it sparingly. I also use repetitive patterns and colors. When applying the principles of scale and proportion, I achieve visual balance and a wow factor in my finished designed spaces.

How can lighting impact a space?
Great lighting adds dimension. It links all the elements by creating an atmosphere. I love interesting lamps and mega chandeliers that make a bold statement. You don't need to light the whole room, you can add ambiance to different areas. Always use a dimmer, especially in multipurpose rooms. Also, know your bulbs. Fluorescent tubes should be avoided at all costs.

Do you have a philosophy or something that you go by as a designer?
Interior design is your personal journey; let your home be an expression of you and your travels.

A well-traveled study for the Columbia Metropolitan Dream Home. Goodwin boasts a collection of vintage furniture and artifacts from her travels.

"My goal with every project is to provide our clients with a space that will allow them to create memories for a lifetime."

Rasheeda Gray

Rasheeda Gray is the founder and lead designer of Gray Space Interiors, a full-service interior design firm based in Philadelphia. After spending fifteen years in marketing and communications, in 2015 she inadvertently lofted her career in interior design. The images of work completed by Gray for her own home would later evolve into a fulfilling career for the designer.

Attention to detail and several other tried and true methods are the cornerstones of modern and chic spaces designed by Rasheeda. Many of the characteristics of her former career play a role in the classic interiors created at Gray Space Interiors. "I'm an unconventional creative. I'm creative, but I'm also very analytical," she says.

How does being a Black designer influence your work?

Being a Black designer influences my work in many different ways. The majority of our clientele at Gray Space is African American, so we see that show up in our work on a cultural level. For example, with artwork, our clients are constantly asking for Black art to not only reflect their stories, but also to support Black artists. Another way is unfolding and telling the stories of our heritage and culture in the art of design.

Let's talk about color. How does it impact a space?

Color is the outline for a design plan, and typically when I'm working on a project, I like to start the project with a source of inspiration, which can come in the form of a piece of art that the client already owns, like pieces collected during travels or a family heirloom. We pull colors from that piece for inspiration. A design trick I typically use: Begin with a primary color throughout the space that represents roughly 50 percent of the color in the room; choose a secondary color which is for approximately 30 percent of the space; last, pick one or two ad-

Rasheeda Gray's "Village" gallery wall in her home's entryway utilizes upcycled frames against a wall painted in Sherwin-Williams Pure White.

The monochromatic palette in Rasheeda Gray's personal living room begins with the pure white wall paint as the background. The plaster-finished fireplace serves as both a source of warmth and a focal point. She created depth in the space with cozy wood elements and plush velvet textures.

"I always choose the paint colors last. There are hundreds of thousands of paint colors, and hundreds of thousands more that can be created with the switch of a formula."

ditional colors as 20 percent of the room. This use of color applies to all elements of the room: walls, furniture, window treatments, construction materials, décor, and more.

How do you bring in the outdoors with your designs?

Of course there's greenery, faux or real. I feel like it brings life to a space. That can be a tall, full plant. It could be a few branches plucked from the garden, placed in the center of a coffee table. It could be a live green wall in a small portion of the kitchen that gets nice natural sunlight. I also like to bring the outside in with some organic textiles or textures or materials. So that could be wood elements: a beautiful mahogany coffee table is just a way to bring nature inside. A fireplace that has sort of a wood slot finish with wood panels is beautiful. If you can have a real fireplace, that's even more like bringing the outside in. I consider the materials that we use in projects to help to bring the outdoors in for sustainability. Being able to bring the outdoors into a space and promoting sustainability are both important.

What's your go-to design trick?

I always choose the paint colors last. There are hundreds of thousands of paint colors, and hundreds of thousands more that can be created with the switch of a formula. A little bit more red, a little less blue, dialing it up 50 percent lighter than the original paint formula. Paint is highly customizable, and so the easiest way to select paint is to select the color from your design plan. If you have a room totally designed out, you can then go and say, "Okay, what color from this design plan do I want to be on the walls?" That's why I always select paint last, because it's highly customizable, your possibilities are endless, and you can select colors from your existing design plan.

What do you want people to remember about you?

I would say that I designed from the soul and my work is much more than a project to me. It is my passion, but also my purpose in life. My goal with every project is to provide our clients with a space that will allow them to create memories for a lifetime. I'm honored to be able to have a career that has that kind of impact.

OPPOSITE TOP LEFT: Greenery, whether real or faux or just in the print of a fabric, brings life to a space. OPPOSITE TOP RIGHT: The graphic wallpaper is from Phillip Jeffries. OPPOSITE BOTTOM LEFT: The modern chandelier is from Z Gallerie, the console is from Hooker Furniture, and the Lucite lamp is by Uttermost. OPPOSITE BOTTOM RIGHT: Chic and whimsical powder room with wallpaper by Kitty McCall for Milton and King, art by Natalie Osborne.

Elaine Griffin is what many consider a pioneer for designers of color in the interior design industry. The nationally recognized tastemaker has created luxurious and timeless interiors for over two decades, while also prioritizing the disruption of the hierarchy of the design industry. "For my industry peers, I hope to be remembered as a trailblazer," Elaine says. "When I began my design career, there were only five (5!!!) Black designers we ever saw in the media. Nationally. I knew God was opening doors for me, and I always sought to remind editorial gatekeepers and industry stakeholders that not all talented designers were blond-haired and blue-eyed."

Throughout her career, Griffin has collected accolades across all kinds of media. Her innate talent as a designer gained her many honors only a few years into establishing her own firm, including as the first African American contributing editor for *Elle Decor*, the first designer of color to participate in the Kips Bay Show House, and the first African American recipient of the New York School of Interior Design's honorary doctorate.

Thoughtfully layering texture and different materials into spaces is just one of the many cornerstones of her design work. She advises, "Vary finishes (painted, natural wood, metal-leafed, ceramic; glossy, satin, and matte) to achieve decor nirvana, even in a minimalist space. It's texture (and not color) that gives a room warmth; color merely sets the ambiance. The more textured elements a room has, the cozier it feels."

"To me, no room is complete without a wee splash of a citrus color as an accent. Yellows, oranges, and corals, decorative infusions of golden sunlight, are universal pops that cross the style spectrum."

Elaine Griffin

How did you get into design?
Interior design is my second career—I was a publicist for nine years in New York City and Paris after I graduated from Yale. I called my mother in Georgia after I got into a huge, very *Devil Wears Prada*–style fight with my *Vogue* editor, and, after listening to my (wine-fueled) wailing, she drawled, "Sugar, why don't you take a hobby and make it your job?"

A minimal seating area with red accents and a Saber-leg side table by T.H. Robsjohn-Gibbings. The enamel and oil canvas is by John Zinnser.

This Westchester living room,
flooded with soft natural
light and neutral tones, was
designed for fashion
executive Bonnie Pressman.

"I'm a fan of organic accessories for bringing the outdoors in—flowers, natural leaves and branches, houseplants, trees, and found objects like seashells and driftwood for the coast; decorative birch logs or vintage antlers for the mountains; and woven wicker, rattan, and bamboo boxes and tables for the city. It's an easily added layer of style and pretty that reminds us where we are."

I enrolled at the New York School of Interior Design immediately. My first job in the design industry was as assistant to the senior architect at Peter Marino.

Let's talk about color. How does it impact a space?
Color reigns supreme in the designer's toolbox, with unparalleled impact. Humans' innate reactions to color dictate our initial response to a space, more so than its contents. (This is why no yellow room will ever be perceived as gloomy.) To me, no room is complete without a wee splash of a citrus color as an accent. Yellows, oranges, and corals, decorative infusions of golden sunlight, are universal pops that cross the style spectrum.

How does lighting impact a space?
Pay attention to your lighting. Honey, if your lighting game isn't together, your room isn't done! Here's what you need to know: All four corners of a space should be lit by their own lamps to avoid dark zones. Floating seating groups need dedicated, eye level-ish lighting when people are both seated and standing. (Eye-level lighting visually defines the zone as you approach.) I'm also into wall washer lighting, or directional recessed lighting, to direct the eye to key design elements like art, a corner, a fireplace, etc. Fact: You could sit lamps on cardboard boxes in an empty room and have killer ambience. Lighting matters.

How do you bring in the outdoors with your designs?
I'm a fan of organic accessories for bringing the outdoors in—flowers, natural leaves and branches, houseplants, trees, and found objects like seashells and driftwood for the coast; decorative birch logs or vintage antlers for the mountains; and woven wicker, rattan, and bamboo boxes and tables for the city. It's an easily added layer of style and pretty that reminds us where we are.

What about focal points?
Focal points anchor a room and make it feel settled. They're visually dominant destinations upon which the eye is meant to rest: the wall behind a sofa, a fireplace, dramatic windows, the area directly across from a room's entrance (which should always have a gorgeous visual moment, FYI). Diana Vreeland legendarily said, "the eye must wander." A room's focal point is the kickoff of that little journey.

What do you want people to remember about you?
If I managed to inspire just one young'un, it was worth it. I live to open doors for others. It makes my heart sing that Black Interior Designers, Inc. (BID) is continuing my late bestie Kimberly Ward's work and is just going gangbusters. #Work! For the design aficionados everywhere, I hope to be remembered as that "designer girl next door" who demystified design and gave them tools to get the look they were after, without all the gobbledygook pretense that many design pros affect.

OPPOSITE TOP: Camel corduroy chairs sourced by Elaine Griffin in Paris circa 2008 from Matignon, the French White House. OPPOSITE BOTTOM: The designer's former Harlem brownstone showcases an original oak mantel and classic bay windows. The deep olive wall color is Sargent by Ralph Lauren.

"A space that is gorgeous but not livable serves no one. We always begin by determining how the space will be used."

Lorna Gross

For Lorna Gross' design projects, telling the story of her clients and the lives they want to live in their home is the cornerstone of each design. Through her North Bethesda, Maryland–based firm, Lorna tackles both residential and commercial design projects, keeping functionality and beauty top-of-mind.

How do you implement the use of texture in your designs?

Layering is one of the things I'm best known for, and I love to use various textures to give warmth and character to a space. Great design is about what we see, but it also should address the other four senses. What we touch and feel is so important to how we enjoy the space we occupy. When I'm creating a concept, I consider fabrics, rugs, stone, metal, and a host of other textures.

How can functionality impact a space?

In design school, we are taught to analyze spaces for function (and safety) first. Then we can make them beautiful. A space that is gorgeous but not livable serves no one. We always begin by determining how the space will be used. A room might be used primarily for reading, watching TV, entertaining, working from home or just gathering. Once I have those answers, I problem-solve for things like acoustics, circulation and even durability for a family with kids or pets. Once all of the functional needs are addressed, we apply all of the fabulous bells and whistles.

Do you have a design philosophy or something that you go by as a designer?

My design approach is based in individualization and dynamic design. I source and incorporate rare elements into the design for a project so that the client's space is highly personalized. I am definitely averse to "cookie cutter" and I love including pieces or details that make a visitor say, "Wow! I wonder where they found that." If we have captured the client's essence, exceeded their expectations, and if the design is difficult to duplicate, I consider that project a success.

Lorna Gross pictured at the Century Furniture showroom in the Washington Design Center.

Amber Guyton is the founder of Georgia-based design firm Blessed Little Bungalow. She is best known for cozy interiors that boast bold, bright pops of color and texture. "When I first meet clients, I ask about their favorite colors and patterns, those they dislike, and what colors exist in their home or life that make them feel good," Amber says. "From that assessment, I am able to design a space with color that reflects those positive emotions I wish to generate in the space."

While color is something her spaces are never lacking (don't hire her if you want a neutral design, she jokes), Amber is equally focused on creating a textural experience. She continues, "Texture is very important. I love layering on different textures with rugs, bedding, pillows, and throws. When building a design, it's important to utilize different textures that will add comfort, but also complement one another, whether wood, fabric, or an art piece. I also love adding texture and dimension to spaces with wallcoverings and millwork."

Amber's design philosophy is simple: She believes that everyone deserves to dwell in a space that relieves, excites, and inspires them. "I like the spaces I design to feel warm and collected, not cold and staged. Layering in different furniture pieces, colors, patterns, textures, and decor gives a room authenticity and its own magic."

How did you get into design?

Since I was a child, I've always enjoyed decorating and rearranging my bedroom, and this continued into adulthood with my dorm rooms, apartments, and houses. In 2016, after I decorated my entire new bungalow within a week of closing, my family and best friends encouraged me to "do this for real." Motivated by that phrase, my business was born. Since then, I've helped dozens of clients design and fall in love with their homes across the United States.

"Remember that opposites attract and don't be afraid to mix the unexpected to make the space more memorable."

Amber Guyton

The guest suite in Amber Guyton's Georgia home showcases artwork by Rachel Stewart Art and a mirror from Nadeau Furniture. A Jungalow rug for Loloi adds a layer of playfulness when paired with the mid-century West Elm chair and lush pink pillows from Modish Decor Pillows.

"Scale is truly do-or-die in design. What's the point of spending thousands of dollars on that gorgeous, comfortable sofa you love if it doesn't fit in the space?"

Do you have a trusted design tip you use often?

I use painter's tape for everything. To plan where to hang art and picture frames; as a straightedge, level, or point of reference; as a measuring tool; and to secure items temporarily. I like to eyeball and ponder on visuals in the moment, so rolls of blue painter's tape are used for that, more than for protecting baseboards and creating clean edges when I am actually painting.

What about lighting?

Updating lighting can completely transform a space, change a room's design style and what decade it appears to be in, modify colors, and shift the mood. I like to swap out builder-basic ceiling fans and add visual interest with bold chandeliers. My advice would be to invest in quality lighting and be mindful of bulb color temperatures (e.g., warm white vs. daylight), as they can drastically affect how a space looks and feels.

How does contrast play a role in a space?

Adding contrast can help any space make an impact. I like to do so with color by creating a complementary color scheme that combines shades from opposite sides of the color wheel. Most of my projects are filled with contrasting moments, like hanging a piece of art with crisp white matting and gold framing against a pitch-black textured wall or placing an orange sofa on top of a navy blue–patterned Moroccan rug. Remember that opposites attract, and don't be afraid to mix the unexpected to make the space more memorable.

Is sustainability important in your designs?

I try my best to source ethical and sustainable products for my clients and for my own home. I also consider the lifespan of a product and see if it can stand the test of time without having to be quickly replaced. To help do your part, I encourage you to research your retailers and see where they stand on fair trade and sustainability. This small effort can make a big difference in how the industry affects our world.

What about movement?

When you get it right, it can make a huge difference. I like to create movement with lighting and drapery that make the eye climb, and patterned wallpaper or rugs that pull you into and around a space. I recommend defining the ideal flow you wish for the room to have and adding elements of movement that will encourage that visually stimulating journey.

What do you want people to remember about you?

I want people to remember how my colorfully designed spaces brought so many people joy. Whether they live in a home I transformed for them or just admire my projects on Instagram, I want my designs to make people feel good, smile, be courageous with color, and think bigger.

This Atlanta photography studio welcomes clients with a rich leather sofa from Wayfair and coffee table and end tables from Nadeau Furniture, flanked by a modern gold floor lamp from HomeGoods.

For Linda Hayslett, a room that isn't layered with design elements like texture and lighting can feel utilitarian—not a place where someone would want to linger. Layering, whether for comfort or dramatic effect, is a skill she has honed well, beginning with her extensive background in another creative realm: fashion.

"This is a second career for me," Linda says. "I went back to school for interior design at FIDM (Fashion Institute of Design & Merchandising) in downtown LA. After I got my degree in design, I knew I wanted to have my own business and company, so I started LH.Designs."

Linda layers color and texture to design spaces with impact, not unlike building a look in fashion. There's a time to add elements to the look, and a time to stop. And just as fashion reflects the style and personality of the wearer, interior design (in Linda's eyes) reflects the homeowner. She keys in on her clients' personalities and lifestyles to get to the essence of how their home should support them and feel.

One of the biggest players in a room's overall atmosphere is texture, she says. "Texture is there to help with the sense of touch and sight. When you have an interesting finish or a soft hand to a design element, that stands out and helps to layer the space [and] create an experience for people when they enter a room. It is *so* important to have texture, and not just flat space, to make a room interesting."

"For too long, society has operated as if being Black means you don't have high standards or your taste is not sophisticated."

Linda Hayslett

How does being a Black designer influence your work?

I'm able to help Black families by understanding their goals, needs, and wants: For too long society has operated as if being Black means you don't have high standards and your taste is not sophisticated. A goal in my projects is to show that I'm at a high level and that my client's home will be, too.

This 5,200-square-foot new-construction home in Hermosa Beach, California, was completed with quartz countertops from Pental, Dacor appliances, and Delta plumbing fixtures.

This kitchen design was inspired by the warmth of farmhouse interiors and mid-century lines. The renovated space was enlarged to three times the size of the original kitchen.

"Plum, maroon, citrus, and mustard colors are always blooming in nature so it's great to also use these shades to make a design statement."

What's your go-to design trick?

Keep it simple for clients. What I mean by that is, our world is changing and becoming faster by the day with technology, and people are becoming less and less patient when it comes to waiting for things. So I don't like to make the design process complicated or detach myself from a project because something is not my part in the process. Once I'm on board for a project, then I'm there to do all the complex things behind the scenes, so clients get a good experience and amazing space at the end of the project.

How do you bring in the outdoors with your designs?

Nature's colors are so beautiful that I like to draw on neutral tones of greens, browns, tans, and blues, and the hues of flowers that blossom and pop against those soft colors. Plum, maroon, citrus, and mustard colors are always blooming in nature, so it's great to also use these shades to make a statement.

How do you get to know clients and their lives to begin creating their space? What's your process like?

I send a questionnaire of about 30-plus questions, depending on the project. This questionnaire dives into not only what the client may want in the project, but what their habits, wishes, and wants are in life. This helps me to get a sense of their current lifestyle and what they hope to create for the future. Once I see their answers, I start a Pinterest board where we both can pin and comment on items. After that, I start figuring out a layout for the space, based on what I'm seeing.

Is scale a factor in your designs?

Scale is always a factor: If pieces aren't the right size, it can really make a room feel off. It's important to know how things will fit in a room. I'm always thinking about how the balance of pieces will play out.

What about focal points?

All rooms should have a focal point. They create a wow factor. If there's nothing that commands attention and creates an experience, people will not absorb the true potential of their environment.

Do you have a design philosophy?

I believe that a space should always be a great experience that enhances a person's mood or life. Making that happen doesn't occur with [just] any vision, it happens with the right vision.

What do you want people to remember about you?

I want people to remember me as a designer who created spaces where amazing experiences occurred and memories were made. That my designs weren't just to make a nice home, but to really create a different approach in how design can be produced.

OPPOSITE TOP LEFT: This modern staircase, with its custom railing and private area for the family pet, is the perfect blend of good looks and functionality. OPPOSITE TOP RIGHT: The seating area in this Long Beach, California, home combines farmhouse texture and mid-century lines. OPPOSITE BOTTOM LEFT AND RIGHT: The fireplace was redesigned and treated with a custom paint (formulated from three colors) to mimic the look of concrete. The same finish is featured as an accent wall in one of the home's bedrooms.

"I love to paint all walls, trims, and moldings the same color. Painting the moldings and trims gives a touch of modern youthfulness to a space."

André Jordan Hilton

For as long as André Jordan Hilton can remember, he has noticed how design made him feel in various rooms throughout his life. One of the most pivotal factors for him in creating a memorable and soothing room has been a careful color selection—even in his own home.

"I've always been intrigued by color and how it impacts a space," André notes. "In my first home, I painted every room a different color. I used bright greens in the living area, which created an inviting feeling of serenity and happiness. I painted the kitchen red, and it felt like I was in an intimate restaurant (a dated one). The bedroom was painted white, with hints of neutral accessories, which created a relaxed, calming, and restful space. In my next home I fell for a trend and painted the walls all gray. It made me feel sad, gloomy, depressed, and lacking motivation, which I hated. After four months of suffering, I decided to paint the entire home Benjamin Moore Simply White, and used bold pops of color in the upholstery, like navy blue and olive green. I also incorporated vibrant art, creating a gallery feel. I felt alive again and excited to walk in my home every day."

The impact this had on André's mood was so powerful to him that he makes sure to discuss color in all of his client consultations. Asking them how they want to feel, room to room, helps him design spaces that feel right.

Even after choosing the perfect color for a room, André believes that establishing a focal point should not be forgotten. "No matter how much drama there is in a room, I always want the eyes to rest on something," he says. "Each space has to have its own moment where something is the center of attention. I utilize artwork, sculptures, or an unusual-shaped furniture piece to draw the eye to that space. Think of it as a point of conversation and interest, or that one thing that tells the complete story of the room itself."

A nature-inspired staircase designed by Andre Hilton for the 2021 Atlanta Holiday Showhouse mixes clean lines and vintage character for a serene, refined space.

"I adore serene spaces and go by the practice that rooms need to breathe in order for even the most formal spaces to feel comfortable and inviting."

How does being a Black designer influence your work?

Although we are growing, we are still rare in the interior design industry. We oftentimes have to go above and beyond to be seen in this field. I push myself harder with each project, gaining as much knowledge and as many resources as I possibly can to elevate my designs. I don't settle for average or mediocre within my work and always find myself stretching my creative abilities beyond the bar set from my previous projects.

What's your go-to design trick?

I love to paint all walls, trims, and moldings the same color. I don't like a lot of contrast when it comes to walls and love a clean canvas to play on. I want all of the focus on the furniture and accessories. I know you're wondering, "Won't you lose the beauty of the moldings?" The answer is no. Details are still details regardless of color. Painting the moldings and trims gives a touch of modern youthfulness to a space, even in a traditional home. This little detail is always a major hit. I also like to mix pieces of furniture, accessories, and art from different time periods. This trick adds character and pushes my clients to be more spontaneous.

How do you get to know clients and their lives to create their space? What's your process like?

Design is a form of psychology to me. During my consultations, I dig into my clients lives by going into their closets. Since clothing choices are so intimate and people wear what makes them feel good, closets tell you a lot about a person. Primary and secondary color choices, fabrics and finishes, room jewelry like chandeliers and vases; you can learn from a simple closet tour. Secondly, I get into their daily routines by spending time with their families and understanding what they do for a living, how often they entertain, the size of their families, and the age range of their children. It is vital to give clients what they need as much as what they want.

Do you have a design philosophy or something that you go by as a designer?

Design for it to be *iconic*.

What do you want people to remember about you?

I want to be known as one of the many iconic Black interior designers that paved the way for the younger generation of Black designers and others to come. Don't be afraid, despite the odds against you, you can do it, too!

This gentleman's grooming lounge was designed for the Junior League of Detroit Showhouse and features Kravet wallpaper and art by Joe Turner.

"I believe that life is better with great design and that a well designed home is a sanctuary that can renew us each day."

Laura Hodges

Laura Hodges Studio is a boutique design firm based in Baltimore and Washington, DC. Laura is a LEED and GREEN AP certified interior designer who specializes in sustainability across all elements of design, from sourcing furniture to recycling existing building materials for construction.

Let's talk about color. How does it impact a space?
I think color is very important in design planning because it impacts your overall experience with your environment and how you feel in a space. We all react differently to specific colors and understanding how you respond, both physically and emotionally, can help you create an environment that perfectly suits your aesthetic.

What about texture?
When designing a space I intuitively incorporate biophilic elements, specifically those that speak to how we interact with our environments. Textures that encourage touch and discovery are an essential layer of the design, creating a cohesive and holistic experience.

How do you incorporate lighting in your designs?
Good lighting is key to making sure that a beautiful space is enjoyed by all, whether you want to feel calm and relaxed or focused and productive. I love to combine ambient, overhead light with sconces at eye level, and table and floor lamps for softer, evening light or task oriented lighting. I reserve recessed lights for kitchens, bathrooms and laundry rooms and use layers of decorative fixtures for living areas.

Do you have a design philosophy or something that you go by as a designer?
Beautifully designed spaces welcome us, surprise us with their thoughtful details, and support a more balanced life. I believe that life is better with great design and that a well designed home is a sanctuary that can renew us each day. Good design is sustainable, so I work toward making design choices that support both our environment and our health.

OPPOSITE TOP: Laura Hodges fully upgraded this builder-grade Baltimore loft with a new kitchen. She traded concrete floors for refined white oak. The counter stools were customized by the designer while she finished the space with abstract BB LaMartina artwork from the client's personal art collection. OPPOSITE BOTTOM: This penthouse boasts beautiful views of downtown. To balance all the reclaimed wood and maintain the views, Laura opted for unique vintage pieces, low-slung sofas, and jewel tones to bring color into the space. The sculptural vintage chairs are from 1stDibs, and the woven tray was designed by Laura for Kazi Goods and handmade in Uganda.

"I choose to use neutral color palettes as the foundation of my design. That provides a balanced, modern base in a room and allows pops of color to breathe in the overall design."

Breegan Jane

Breegan Jane, a lifestyle expert, designer, and HGTV host, believes that luxury is attainable at any price point—that it is more of an aesthetic than a price tag. But luxury, at the end of the day, is not a perk when the design is nice to look at but doesn't serve the homeowner's needs for daily life.

"I've had the opportunity to work on luxurious spaces over 41,000 square feet," she says. "I've also designed one-bedroom apartments. Both were designed with luxury in mind. I make sure the visual appeal aligns with how everything functions best for clients. Pretty without purpose is a waste, in my opinion. There are so many ways to create opulence in home decor: hints of gold, quality upholstery, personalized accents. Everyone can enjoy sophistication in their spaces."

Through her design firm she blends a philanthropic core with helping others design homes that are simple, serene, and comfortable. Her passion for helping others (exhibited while serving as an example of an entrepreneurial single mom on a personal scale and through her role on the TV show *Extreme Makeover: Home Edition* on a national level) naturally translates to the spaces she creates for clients.

Utilizing texture to incorporate warmth, neutral palettes that promote balance, and strategic scale, Breegan works to forge interiors that can be described as modern, attainable, and luxurious.

How does being a Black designer influence your work?

I remember going on a field trip to Colonial Williamsburg when I was very young. My classmates and I were shown the differences in living quarters of enslaved people versus colonists. The grave disparity made such an impression on my young mind. Even today, as a biracial, transracially adopted woman living in a place where wealth and pov-

A Southern California office inspired by modern lines and rich materials. A vintage stone statue rests behind the desk. Breegan Jane created the chairs to mirror the rug's color and created space for the gold accessories to pop. The fireplace anchors the room with deep orange and brown hues.

> *"I can put 100 beautiful things in a room, but without a clear focal point, it's just a room with visual cacophony. Nothing is unique or special, and the entire space will be overwhelming."*

erty aren't assigned to any one race, those memories remain vivid. I believe every person, regardless of ethnic makeup or background, deserves to live in a place that is functional, beautiful, clean, and safe. My design will always be influenced by who I am, because I embrace all of who I am, and I bring all of myself to every project I endeavor.

How do you bring in the outdoors with your designs?

Because I'm a working mom who's always on the go, I incorporate a mix of real and faux plants in my home decor. Strategically placing them near windows creates a visual flow between my indoor and outdoor spaces. Likewise, lighting plays a big part of spatial planning in my designs. I'm a huge fan of skylights and incorporating natural light as much as possible in home projects. I've also put actual outdoor furniture in my home for my sons to use. It's very durable, and I've been able to profile it in a way that most would never know it's outdoor furniture.

What about focal points?

It's important when designing a space that you create a calmness to direct your eye. I can put 100 beautiful things in a room, but without a clear focal point, it's just a room with visual cacophony. Nothing is unique or special, and the entire space will be overwhelming.

Do you have a design philosophy or something that you go by as a designer?

My professional creativity focuses on designing for a life lived honestly. Design should absolutely and always be beautiful. However, it should also be tailored to how you use your space and be infused with your lifestyle, preferences, and daily needs. The function and flow of your interior design should be as important as the overall appearance and aesthetic. That means incorporating stylish storage, accessible must-haves, and realistic decor/design, as just a few examples.

What do you want people to remember about you?

I believed in myself, but part of my motivation was to pave the way for others. It was uncomfortable building my business, especially when everyone was telling me I wouldn't be able to do it as a single mother. However, I did it because I believed I could, but also because I wanted to play quarterback for others coming behind me who believed they could do the same thing. I hope people remember me as an example of determination. I got up on the hard days and did the hard things to remind others to get up on the hard days and do the hard things. It's possible, and it's worth it.

This luxury dining room combines an assortment of vintage gold mirrors from Chairish with a new linear chandelier and gold-accented dining table from Restoration Hardware.

"If you're not going to use color to give a space layers, using various textures becomes all the more important to give the project visual depth."

Corey Damen Jenkins

Corey Damen Jenkins aims to design spaces that exude sophisticated comfort. The Detroit-born interior designer has a true affinity for creating luxurious yet livable layers in the spaces he designs. "I never want the projects I design to have an expiration date," Corey says. "By giving each interior design some derivative of what I call, 'The Fresh Continental Mix,' my ultimate goal is that clients' homes always feel relevant, classically elegant, approachable, and comfortable."

His more-is-more use of color, texture, and pattern has awarded him notable accolades and TV appearances. In addition to New York, where he resides, Jenkins has designed spaces globally, leaving his stamp in Hawaii, Nantucket, Saudi Arabia, and many other places.

"As a maximalist, I want our firm's design work to be remembered for creating the tension point where modernity and antiquity meet, and for wielding color and pattern in an unapologetic, fashion-forward way."

How did you get into design?
After being laid off from a successful career in the automotive industry, I launched our design firm during the Great Recession, in 2009. I searched for my first clients by literally knocking on 779 householders' doors in the suburban neighborhoods of Detroit, Michigan, in the dead of winter. The clients at the 779th door were very kind and gave me three spaces to decorate. As our relationship flourished, they eventually awarded the entire home's design and decoration scope to my one-man company. After completing their project, I had the interiors professionally photographed and posted the images on my website. Two weeks later, my work was discovered online by casting executives at HGTV, who eventually cast me on my first television show. It was a reality competition series, and I was named the winner. Shortly after that national exposure, it was time to staff up!

How do you use color in your designs?
Think of color like a softball: You can toss a softball to someone in such a way that they catch it and appreciate it, or you can hurl it at them with such force that it knocks them down. Similarly, color should always be used judiciously, because it's such a powerful element that it is truly transformative in interior spaces. It can transport even the most mundane rooms to the realms of the wow, but only when it's deployed thoughtfully and with precision. Garish usage of color distracts and destroys.

Why is layering important?
Layering spaces with decorative accessories provides viewers with justification to let their eyes rove and roam, to discover more about the person who resides in that home. The walls should be adorned with art choices that make you think, and *objets d'art* that portray the owner's obsessions, beliefs, and world travels. Such things needn't be expensive or flashy, but they should tell a cohesive story.

Do you have a trusted design tip you use often?
Never ignore the design opportunities provided by ceilings.

Corey Jenkins, photographed in the 2021 Dallas Kips Bay Decorator Show House, with its Louis XVI chairs from 1stDibs, a custom Cambria quartz dining table, fully draped walls created by the Shade Store with Sanderson fabric, and Versailles parquet floors.

"Layering spaces with decorative accessories provides viewers with justification to let their eyes rove and roam, to discover more about the person who resides in that home."

Do you have any advice on using texture?

Texture can give a room depth and warmth. It's important that fabric choices are not one-note, especially as pertains to window treatments, furniture, rugs, etc. You should diversify the hand of fabric at work within your design by employing chenille, velvets, silk, linens, and blends. Mix it up and always keep functionality top of mind. This is especially crucial when decorating rooms with neutral color palettes: If you're not going to use color to give a space layers, using various textures becomes all the more important to give the project visual depth.

What about pattern?

Contrary to what some may believe, the key to using patterns effectively in a space is actually not about excess—it's all about exercising restraint. Even a room that is heavily driven with lots of maximalist patterns should be governed by a certain level of editing: knowing when to utilize large-scale patterns, juxtaposing them against smaller scale choices, or forgoing certain pattern choices altogether. For example, a very elaborate Heriz rug can carry a sofa that's upholstered in a solid fabric, or in a very intense chintz, or even in a pinstripe. It all depends on the scale of the patterns and textures involved and knowing when to go big and when to stop.

In this stunning parlor, Corey Jenkins set the tone with rich chocolate walls. The space is softened with white, green, and cream furnishings and art, while the repurposed settee adds a grand pattern and texture to the room.

A Marvel-inspired kids' lounge.

"I've learned through design that we seek who and what we are through our lived experience."

General Judd

General Judd abides by a design ethos that is rooted in an essentialism layered with life and a good dose of rich hues and textures. As one half of Me and General Designs (his wife, Cristina Casañas, is the other half), Judd combines a lifelong affinity for well-designed homes with his TV, film, and theater experience. He is a member of Benjamin Moore's Designer Alliance and is deliberate in his use of color, especially through paint. "Color is magic! Moody, quiet, exciting, whimsical. So many offerings and so much impact!"

Me and General Designs births spaces that are meant to elevate the human experience for each and every client. "I've learned, through design, that we seek who we are through our lived experience: life can be serene, but it still has multiple layers."

How did you get into design?
Growing up in Charlotte, North Carolina, I was always drawing and would thumb through magazines with my mother, dreaming of living in these luxurious homes. This piqued my interest into design and created a passion for a better life. I was fortunate to hone my design skills in the art department on many film and television productions. I met my wife and business partner after moving to New York (I was in "Blue Man Group" off-Broadway; she was a film and TV set decorator). We combined our experience and design vision to create Me and General Design, shaping lifestyles rather than just setting the scene.

Do you use focal points in your designs?
We create an overall cohesive design, then add art or a custom element to draw you in. Our spaces offer many focal points, depending on where you are in the room.

Do you follow a design philosophy?
We consciously design interior environments to elevate the human spirit!

What do you want people to remember about you?
I strived to move humanity forward through life and design.

OPPOSITE TOP: The family-friendly home lounge features graphic wallpaper from Phillip Jeffries; sleek stools from Mark Jupiter; modern and playful tile from Fireclay; *Señorita Hummingbird*, a print by Dolan Geiman; and a SWICK Board speaker by Me and General Design. OPPOSITE BOTTOM: A modern, monochromatic outdoor lounge area equipped for entertaining.

Brooklyn-based interior designer Delia Kenza uses inspiration from the lasting impression of her grandmother's elegance to create interiors that are modern interpretations of the past. With a mid-century and vintage-curated aesthetic, Delia promotes sustainability by using vintage pieces as decor. She feels that the use of sustainable products is necessary when designing a room, not only for the sake of aesthetics, but for the planet. Vintage pieces like heirloom mementos and passed-down artwork layer a space with history and make the room feel like it has evolved over time—something Delia seeks to achieve with each design project.

Delia brings rooms to life with her strategic use of lighting, color, and art. She says, "Color has a significant impact on space. It has the power to evoke moods and emotions. I am very intentional about my use of color and tend to gravitate toward rich, moody tones."

"Art . . . goes beyond the canvas and can be in the form of furniture, lighting, sculpture, etc."

Delia Kenza

How does being a Black designer influence your work?

I don't let race influence my work. However, through my experience of being a person of color in America who travels internationally, my point of view has fully expanded. My travels make me more aware and sensitive to other cultures. I strive to create culturally accurate spaces because your home should reflect who you are.

Why is it important to layer a room?

Layers create interest and add depth. The best rooms are layered with history. Incorporating vintage pieces or beloved treasures and heirlooms brings personality and dimension.

This home in Clinton Hill, New York, has been in Delia Kenza's family for generations. Delia elected to keep much of the original architecture in place while using a mix of contemporary and vintage finds to create depth. The wall sculpture is by Júlio Leitão. The wood accent chair is from Estudio Persona, and the coffee table is a vintage find from Maurice Villency.

What about texture?

Interior design should impact all of your senses. Texture brings warmth and comfort to a space. Texture, of course, can be found in soft furnishings but also in art, plants, and accessories as they all add texture, color, and depth.

How do you bring in the outdoors with your designs?

Simply having access to a fire escape balcony lets you enjoy the sun and grow flowers. Window treatments can bring in the outdoors, too: Framing a window with beautiful curtains captures the beauty of your outdoor view.

OPPOSITE LEFT: Brooklyn living room. Art by Daniel Heidkamp. Vintage stools were recovered in curly sheepskin. ABOVE: Muted patterns and neutral textures create subtle moodiness in this serene bedroom.

Do you have a trusted design tip you use often?

Rooms should grow, and the best spaces evolve over time, or look like they did. I also love to add some black: even a little brings depth and weight to a room.

How do you use lighting?

Incoprorating many sources—overhead and wall lighting, floor and table lamps—is key.

Any tips on artwork?

I encourage my clients to buy art that they love, not just art that matches the room. You should love the art you hang around your home, and support new artists. Art also goes beyond the canvas and can be in the form of furniture, lighting, sculpture, etc.

Do you have a design philosophy you go by?

Have fun, don't be afraid to try, and make sure the space tells a story.

"Sometimes color plays a celebratory, symbolic, or historical role in design, which, for Black people, has always been significant and empowering."

Bailey Li

Bailey Li Interiors is a design firm grounded in innovative uses of color and color applications led by interior artist Alicia Bailey. "The more I came to understand the psychological and spiritual effects of color, I began to honor the importance of intentional color selection in my projects," she shares.

Bailey is a self-proclaimed design rebel whose ethos is centered on exploration that can be experienced through impressive and one-of-a-kind murals, installations, and art. "As I embraced integrating color in my projects, I improvised. I would paint color onto leathers. I have since remained dedicated to sharing with the world how color can be harnessed in interior design."

Let's talk about color. How does it impact a space?

We are all connected to color—from our eyes, hair, the food we eat, our land and marine life, the architecture in our cities—it is everywhere. However, on an abstract but very significant note, color is associated with the science of chakras and the auras of human beings. Many Eastern sciences and spiritual practices teach us that hues can stimulate vibratory frequencies to awaken and heal us. Sometimes color plays a celebratory, symbolic, or historical role in design, which, for Black people, has always been significant and empowering. Our connection and integration of color in our homes and commercial spaces tells a story that sustains the true essence of our individuality and communities. I encourage us all to allow color to act as a superpower in our interiors.

What about texture?

Texture appeals to our sense of touch; it's the "feel-good" element in design. It also goes hand-in-hand with color and light to create an elevated ambiance in two ways: It adds depth and creates a nuanced platform for color and light. For instance, luxurious silk drapery, rich velvet upholstery, or lustrous wood grain are magnetic to our visual senses in isolation. Now, add to this, lighting design—whether natural, incandescent, candlelit, or LED-powered—the textures' enhancement and visual elevation are inevitable when illuminated at certain angles or lumens.

How can lighting impact a space?

Let there be light! One of the reasons I love skylights, floor-to-ceiling windows, and sheer drapery is because of how accommodating they are to natural rays of sunlight. There is a radiance that only the sun can bestow when a space is kissed by its magical beams. The luminaries within a space's design are the stars of show. They guide us in acclimating to an environment, as lighting has the capacity to dictate the level of drama, sophistication, whimsy, or calm we might expect in an atmosphere. Lighting will always be tied to mood as well as function; depending on the use of the space, one may take precedence over the other. A tip to remember: Improper lighting and incompatible color can incite or exacerbate conditions such as depression or irritability, and yet, when applied properly, can uplift an ambiance, encourage harmonious gatherings, and evoke joy and delight in residents, consumers, or other users in various spaces.

Bailey Li shown in her personal boho loft, a restored firehouse. Li reimagined World Market drapery with fashion designer Milele Atelier to create privacy in the open space. An industrial sheet metal–and–leather headboard from Restoration Hardware anchors the space.

"I believe that scale is fundamental in our pursuit of achieving unique interiors overall."

Michael London

Ontario-based interior designer Michael London is focused on giving clients a space that is both immersive and influenced by culture. Michael's designs embody streamlined luxury and stem from a deep-rooted love for design that has been with him since he was young.

Do you have a design philosophy or something that you go by as a designer?

"Beautify the world" is the design philosophy that I go by as an interior designer. My mother, with great insight, knew my calling and told me, "You are going to beautify the world."

Does scale play a factor in your designs?

In designing residences from 4,000 to 18,000 square feet, scale plays an important factor that is evident in our designs and at the forefront in the design process. In small-scale design I focus on detailed elements such as counter edges, unique floor patterns, and hardware detailing. In large-scale design I focus on designing the volume of space with large-scale art, multiple fixtures, and larger focal points. I believe that scale is fundamental in our pursuit of achieving unique interiors overall.

How do color and texture impact a space?

As design on a whole evolves, color is an aspect of design that influences emotion and heightens one's perception of the interior space. I love to create impact by using color palettes in deeper tones, but in ways that push the envelope and keep the home up-to-date, classic, and timeless. Designing a natural-palette interior, while playing up on textures, is one aspect of design I enjoy. Attention to textures like linens, chenille, suede, and leather in the same palettes adds levels of interest, enhancing details and the level of luxury without adding an accent color.

Michael London, pictured in his Lytton Park, Toronto, project. A Bocci 28 Armature light fixture creates a warm focal point, and custom-designed trim work including the casing, backband, and baseboards of the room are finished in Benjamin Moore Silver Satin OC-26.

"[Try] painting the entire room the same color, from walls and border to ceiling. This not only makes a smaller space seem larger, but also showcases your room as a beautiful canvas."

Travis London

For as long as he can remember, Travis London has been enamored of lovely places and grand experiences. "I was born a designer," he says. "Making things beautiful is all I know. As a kid I was always rearranging our house. At sixteen I recreated Gianni Versace's Lake Como bedroom in my bedroom."

Alongside design, food is another prominent passion; Travis ran a successful catering company for years before moving to Paris and later, Milan. In those captivating cities, he cemented his future in interior design. "I was able to explore my love and knowledge of design before launching my own design company, Studio London Co.," Travis says.

Now Travis works to create spaces that are punctuated with saturated colors, bold patterns, and bright personality—bringing a sense of grandeur along to each project.

Let's talk about color. How does it impact a space?
For me a life without color is a life without love. Color changes a space in a huge way because it brings it to life!

Why is it important to layer a room design?
It adds dimension, layers, and personalization to a space. Personalization is what makes a house a home. Adding intricate design elements to a space makes it more personal, truly showcasing and reflecting the personality of its inhabitants.

What's your go-to design trick?
Painting the entire room the same color from walls and border to ceiling. This not only makes a smaller space seem larger, but also showcases your room as a beautiful canvas.

OPPOSITE: Travis London's Miami dining room has a stunning custom chandelier paired with a lavish vintage table and custom-upholstered chairs.

"My mom told me not to care what anyone thinks and to always stay authentic to myself. I follow that rule when designing and in life."

What about texture?

I love texture. I love things you can touch and feel. I love textured walls. I love anything that adds a dimensional element. Texture enriches a space with depth.

How do you get to know clients and their lives to begin creating their space? What's your process like?

My aim is to create deeply meaningful work that reflects the true identity—and most glamorous self—of the homeowner, [and] that energy can be felt in my designs. To do so, I get to know my clients so I can understand who they truly are. Since I am a designer who is known for color, I have to know what colors mean to the client and what feelings and memories they associate with each. I love to start in the closet of my clients and see what colors they wear the most, what colors they wear when wanting to be sexy, playful, strong. Those are all elements I take into account when pulling together the color schemes of the house.

How does being a Black designer influence your work?

Being Black culturally, we are people full of style, and style has always been around us. Growing up, we didn't associate wealth with having actual money; we associated it with having nice things and a nice home. An awareness of the value of design and aesthetics has been with us our whole lives. It has shaped my eye and my views, which is why I am a designer today.

Do you have a design philosophy or something that you go by as a designer?

My mom told me not to care what anyone thinks and to always stay authentic to myself. I follow that rule when designing and in life.

What do you want people to remember about you?

That I loved and lived in color and made people happy through my designs.

OPPOSITE TOP LEFT: Turquoise velvet credenza from Anthropologie and Kendra Dandy original painting of Travis London and his dogs. OPPOSITE TOP RIGHT: A seating nook near the living room includes Scalamandré pink velvet covers on CB2's Gwyneth chairs. The bone-inlay table from CB2 sits below a Jonathan Adler lamp. OPPOSITE BOTTOM LEFT: Sheepskin armchairs from Restoration Hardware, a vintage Italian lamp from 1stDibs, and drop it MODERN wallpaper complete London's home office. OPPOSITE BOTTOM RIGHT: Travis reupholstered the Restoration Hardware sofa in a Scalamandré orange velvet fabric. Flor's Mod Cow rug adds a patterned pop.

"Think about how you want to use the space and ensure that there is appropriate lighting for those activities."

Cheryl Luckett

Cheryl Luckett believes your environment should tell your story, and layers of visual interest help to do just that. "I've become adept at reading the room," Cheryl says. "Often, it's what we see in a home that tells us so much more than what a client says. Existing art, color selections, collectibles, past purchases, etc., often give hints into who they are and allow us to use those possessions as a jumping-off point for our design."

Sometimes a blend of those existing possessions and a fresh new design by way of patterns and space planning can be the best of both worlds: using something of sentimental value to the homeowner while practicing sustainability.

"Stewardship is one of the ways we bring sustainability to our clients," Cheryl notes. "Whether we incorporate their existing pieces into our designs, or we seek out vintage, or source locally from nearby artists and makers, our aim is to be good stewards of our client's resources and our environment."

Cheryl prioritizes the clients and how she can empower them in the spaces they live in with a unique approach that spotlights functionality in all of the design elements of a space.

Do you have a trusted design tip you use often?
Adding vintage elements is one of my go-to tactics for bringing history and interest into a space. We work to create spaces that feel as if their contents were collected and curated over time, and when that's not the case, vintage furnishings and decor can help to create that feeling.

How do you incorporate lighting in your designs?
Lighting is a key element in any space, and the scale, placement, and variety of lighting matter. We use lighting in a way that highlights how a client will use the space. Think about how you want to use the space and ensure that there is appropriate lighting for those activities. A quick call to an electrician to add an outlet or a lighting receptacle can be life changing in terms of how you illuminate and ultimately use a space.

What about pattern?
Pattern is one of my favorite design elements to employ. A successful mix of patterns can instantly elevate a space and give it that "designer" look. When mixing patterns, we typically select a *master fabric* that includes a mix of colors and that is often larger in scale than the other patterns that will be added. This allows us to use that fabric to add on smaller-scale geometric or organic coordinates that tie back to the master. It makes ensuring the right mix so much easier.

Why is art impactful?
Art has the power to completely transform a space. It also speaks directly to the clients and who they are. Even if you're not a true collector, selecting art that represents your interest, values, culture, and journey will help to create a house that feels much more like a home.

Cheryl Luckett with some favorite design elements: "A successful mix of patterns can instantly elevate a space."

A cool and airy space is warmed by a custom-tufted ottoman and salmon velvet armchairs from Rowe Fine Furniture.

"Each space we design is a true reflection of the people who live in it and is thoughtfully crafted to support the way they want to live."

How do you think about functionality?

We encourage clients to begin the design process with function. Determine how you want the space to function, then how you want it to feel, and lastly how you want it to look. It can be easy to skip to how a space should *look*, but there are many ways to a pretty space. You need to first ensure that you're creating one that will work for you.

What about movement?

Flow matters. Visual movement, and also the physical movement of people in a space, are important elements. A plan that works for the intended use of a space can do wonders for increasing function and usability. The default tendency is to place furniture on the walls, but more often than not, pulling the furniture away from the walls will create a much more inviting and livable space.

Do you follow a design philosophy?

We specialize in creating elegant, personalized, life-friendly homes for our clients and their loved ones to enjoy. Each space we design is a true reflection of the people who live in it and is thoughtfully crafted to support the way they want to live. We serve our clients with professionalism, reliability, stewardship, and respect.

What do you want people to remember about you as a designer?

I view design as my ministry, and I take sharing my God-given gifts with others seriously. My aim is and will always be to help create spaces that help empower people to live their best lives, whatever that means for them.

The designer's personal kitchen and breakfast nook features vibrant custom drapery from Robert Allen fabric and a tufted teal banquette designed by Cheryl for Sylvester Alexander.

"When a room has a natural focal point or a unique architectural detail, I try to emphasize that area by adding attention-grabbing design elements around that space."

Don Ricardo Massenburg

No matter who he's designing for, Don Ricardo Massenburg wants home to feel like the final destination, where the personality of the homeowner is shown through both aesthetics and life-improving practicality.

"My goal for every client is to elevate their space, to where beauty and function align, so that they live and feel better in their home or workspace," he says. That alignment of beauty and function can often be overlooked in places like the bedroom, but not by Don. He says that bed styling and layering are his go-to tricks to take a bedroom to the next level.

"I can make a bed look and feel so good that clients can't wait to dive in it, and they don't want to get out of it! A beautifully made bed can make the entire room look and feel amazing. Most questions I get from other designers and home decor enthusiasts are about bed styling and layering tips. I've even had clients ask me to return to their home to make their beds."

That's just one aspect of Don's job that makes his work feel fun, which is something he always wanted out of a career. In his designs, he blends bold and luxurious furnishings and finishes to create rooms that are driven by his natural passion for art and the client's dreams for the space.

How did you get into design?

Although I didn't initially pursue interior design, I knew that my job as a teacher wasn't going to fulfill my yearning for the arts. So I poured my passion into styling my first apartment. I entered photos of that apartment into an online interior design contest hosted by Apartment Therapy. That contest, and the feedback I received, pushed me to pursue interior design as a hobby and then a career. I took interior design courses and worked alongside an upholsterer who taught me the ins and outs of furniture making. I loved upholstery and started to sell

OPPOSITE TOP: A formal living room in Durham, North Carolina, features two-tone walls and warm gold accents. OPPOSITE BOTTOM: Rich materials and comfortable seating align beauty and function in a luxurious bedroom.

"I focus on natural light as a valuable design element. Sunlight can make any room come alive and can also pull out the variations of color in the furniture and fabrics of the space."

fabric headboards and other pieces. When I delivered and installed a bed, I would style the space with pillows and other accessories, and then post the photos on social media and buy/sell/trade sites. From there, the demand shifted from customers only wanting a headboard or upholstery work to people inquiring about full-room design.

How does being a Black designer influence your work?

I strive for excellence as a standard in every step of my process. I create with a boldness that shows that I am unapologetically me and that my work and place in this industry matter today and have always mattered.

Are focal points important?

Focal points create flow and help with balance. When a room has a natural focal point or a unique architectural detail, I try to emphasize that area by adding attention-grabbing design elements around that space. If a space does not have a focal point, it can be created by the way furniture is positioned, art is placed, or where light falls. I like the focal point to immediately catch the eye of the person as they walk into the space, but the other elements complement proportionally so that the eye is encouraged to continue moving around the room. In many of my spaces, the focal point is typically an oversized headboard in a bedroom, a large piece of art, or a beautiful window all decked out in lush drapery panels.

What do you want people to remember about you?

I would love to be remembered as a gentleman who was always kind, open to sharing, and who was in love with interior design.

This neutral North Carolina dining room is wrapped in warm grasscloth wallpaper and creamy gray wainscotting. The Arteriors chandelier and dining table from Universal Furniture add a pleasant, unexpected contrast.

"My favorite material to incorporate texture in a room is wallpaper. You can never go wrong with a good wallpaper in a funky pattern or color."

NeKeia McSwain

NeKeia "Keia" McSwain was enamored with interior design long before pursuing a career in the industry. A natural instinct to upgrade interior spaces is the primary reason her process begins with "courting the client," as she calls it. "Once I've confirmed the respect level, collaborative effort, and, most importantly, willingness to trust the process, the rest is smooth sailing," Keia notes.

Keia designs rooms that are bold, worldly, and oftentimes filled with saturated colors and sophisticated yet fun patterns. "My first mission is always selecting a tenacious color story, then paint and wallpaper color for a space."

Keia operates from a place of intentionality in both her process and design through her studio, NeKeia & Co. Her use of color, texture, and pattern typically sets the tone for the final design of a space. But first defining how the room will be used for highest functionality ensures the best design in the end, she says. "Reading the room is essential," Keia advises. "When reading the room you fully understand the prime use of the space."

How did you get into design?

There wasn't a time when I wasn't aware of my immense love for decor, the home, and how they play such a pivotal role in the everyday lifestyle. A goal in life has always been to beautify my core and remain fresh, current, and strong in my daily evolution. My passion for design and the need to pursue it as a first love was fate. My journey began at age eight with a floral comforter and matching cotton candy–striped wallpaper as the cherry on top. In college I got the Best Dorm Decor award. You know you have a true affinity for something when you visit friends and family only to rearrange their homes and personal spaces. It's always a privilege when they encourage it.

Let's talk about color. How does it impact a space?

Everyone sees color from a different viewpoint. The goal is to understand how certain colors affect certain personality types. Taking a deep dive into the psychology of color and how it affects spaces and their occupants is extremely revealing and eye opening. Color will always be dominant in a space. It creates boldness and a commitment to the space. The key is to be sure you are intentional with placement when using color, down to the finish, shade, and tone.

What about texture?

Texture is often underrated and is a huge provider of balance. It is deserving of respect for its impact in both minimal and quaint spaces and in the most elegant and grand spaces. The depth of a space is a reflection of the textures incorporated. Much of the visual weight a room carries is created through the textural elements of the space. Visual texture allows you the opportunity to see texture without necessarily feeling it. Accents like wainscoting, intentional architecture, and lighting can all add another layer of texture to a space. Wood grain, for

NeKeia McSwain pictured at the New York Design Center.

"Color will always be dominant in a space. It creates boldness and a commitment to the space. The key is to be sure you are intentional with placement when using color, down to the finish, shade, and tone."

example, is swirling with texture while still being generally smooth to the touch. Tactile texture allows you to both feel and see texture under your touch. Pebbled leather is a great example of this, as the texture is both visual and physical. I enjoy incorporating different types of textures into projects to bring them to life. My favorite material to incorporate texture in a room is wallpaper. You can never go wrong with a good wallpaper in a funky pattern or color.

How do you bring in the outdoors with your designs?

Bringing the outdoors into design is a sacred and intentional process. Plants are not only beautiful but functional inside of the home because they improve the overall air quality. Signature plants incorporated into my work are the bird of paradise and the fiddle-leaf fig. Skylights are an awesome way to bring in sunshine to those lush plants while letting more natural light into the space. Earth-toned fabrics, ceramics, and stoneware are great and continue the organic outdoor vibe.

How important are focal points?

I consider the focal point to be quite comparable to the shoes for your outfit, and I normally notice those first. The eye should dance around a space, settling on a focal point to define the area. Creating a fun and direct focal point by incorporating a telling and evoking piece of artwork is always an option. Artwork and the story behind the work is a salient reminder that a space is not complete without artwork or a strong and present focal point. An amazing marble tile or a handwoven silk rug will also do the trick for a subtle resting place within a space. Implementing cool and striking lighting is another great way to create a focal point.

Do you have a design philosophy you go by?

I'll never be truly content with my creativity if I am simultaneously analyzing while creating. Creating, brain dumping, and working through the kinks are not the same processes with which we analyze. It is always ideal to keep this in mind when creating.

What do you want people to remember about you as a designer?

I will be remembered as one of the most fearless interior designers, unpredictable in style, presentation, clientele, and experience. I want my work to have encouraged novice designers to break down barriers while creating their own tailored design aesthetic. I want to be remembered as the woman who saw no barriers and carried along in her backpack an immense and unbreakable love for the interior design industry.

A "Whole Home" showhouse media room. The custom arch by Architectural Grille is finished in Farrow & Ball Bancha, and the tile is from Ann Sacks. The stunning hide wallcovering from Arte creates a soulful and luxurious lounge-inspired space.

The incredibly sultry media room is wrapped in stunning hair-on-hide wallcovering from Arte, with trim and ceilings painted in Farrow & Ball Bancha. Just beyond the main seating area, a gold-and-glass table from Bradley Furniture makes room for conversation.

"We often forget that the spaces we call home need the love and care that you would naturally give someone you care deeply about. When you love up on your home, it loves you right back."

Nike Onile

For Nike Onile, spatial artist and principal designer of the Toronto-based firm Studio Ode, interior design is a second career, which parallels the experiences of many other creatives.

"My journey into the world of design was unconventional," Nike recalls. She considers herself an artist to her core, but she initially pursued a career in life sciences.

"Most second-generation individuals are familiar with parental pressures to select career paths that are 'most likely' to end in success. As a child raised in a traditional Nigerian household, there was not much room for me to deviate from 'the honorable 3'—doctor, lawyer, engineer." So Nike ended up in the health care industry, feeling unfulfilled.

She found momentary relief through painting and sculpting. "When I bought my first place, I did what I did with all my canvases—capture inspiration and fill the space with meaning. This was the start of my interior design career. I didn't go to school for interior design, but for me, the artistic principles are the same when it comes to creating something that moves people. Focus on the story that is worth telling—and tell it in the simplest way. This seemed to resonate with others and before I knew it, I had built a practice around telling three-dimensional stories within the walls of people's homes."

With a primary focus on wellness and space as it functions for the home dweller, Nike creates interiors that are amplifications of the client's lifestyle.

How does being a Black designer influence your work?

For the most part, my identity and experiences influence my work as a designer in the way I connect with people, places, and objects. Since I am always meeting my clients in a moment of transition, my ability to connect to my roots gives me the insight

An open great room with monochromatic patterns and cool accents.

"Adjusting scale, especially when unexpected, adds a sense of playfulness."

to create spaces that inspire wellness. I hold space for others. One may say that I have been training for this my whole life. I was born with this ability to see things a different way, and it took me years to claim my power and realize its value. I spent time silencing the noise, and in this silence is where I create.

Why is it important to layer a room with design elements?

Layering a home is how you add soul to a space. It's where depth comes from, and it really depends on who is living in the home. Because at the end of the day "space" is just the four walls of a room held together by nails. Being clear about what that space represents for you, and what is needed for you to feel supported, makes the difference. We often forget that the spaces we call home need the love and care that you would naturally give someone you care deeply about. When you love up on your home, it loves you right back.

Whether it's a piece of furniture passed down through generations, art created by a loved one, or a chair wrapped in the cloth of your country, no matter the design aesthetic, soul is your home's love language and each piece in your space tells a story.

What's your go-to design trick?

My favorite equation for adding character to a home while using the senses is by playing with scale, contrast, and texture. This combination always seems to create excitement, even in the most basic dwellings. Texture has a way of making a space feel abundant. Adjusting scale, especially when unexpected, adds a sense of playfulness. Contrast has a way of drawing your eye in and creating incredible focal points. I find that tweaking this trio in various ways is a foolproof method to create major impact in any space.

Do you have a design philosophy or something that you go by as a designer?

To create a space that feels full, all the senses must be nourished. We spend most of our lives and an incredible amount of our energy in the spaces we live and work in, so it is only natural that we create space that supports us in a way that makes us feel brilliant. The value here is creating a safe space that pours back into us. One that is not only functional, but is set up to foster health, inspiration, and a richness of life.

What do you want people to remember about you?

The spaces I create are all focused around a sense of wellness and a complete indulgence of the senses. Fifty years from now, I'd like people to think, "spaces that evoke emotion," when they think about my work.

OPPOSITE TOP LEFT: The living room in the Legends JW Marriott private residence. OPPOSITE TOP RIGHT: An intimate dining room with organic layers. OPPOSITE BOTTOM LEFT: Minimalist kitchen designed by Nike Onile. OPPOSITE BOTTOM RIGHT: Dining room for a private residence at the JW Marriott in Edmonton, Alberta, designed by Onile and Jena Nasser.

Community, a vegan restaurant
in Oakville, Ontario.

David Quarles IV is a Memphis-based designer with a philosophy deeply rooted in creating happiness in all areas of the client's life, specifically in the home. "I feel that happiness starts at home, and our homes are where we recharge our happiness."

Interiors produced by David are often bursting with color. "My experience with color is a little bit different just because I am a synesthete with chromesthesia, which means my brain associates color with music. As I'm listening to a song, it's almost as if I am in a colorful kaleidoscope. I use that to help my clients who may not be able to tell me exactly what they want out of a space, and so I'll ask them, 'What is your favorite song or what is the playlist that you imagine yourself listening to in this space?' This helps me translate textures and colors that they want to use."

As a designer of African American, Afro-Caribbean, European, and Indigenous American descent, David is always looking to his culture as a source of inspiration while working on projects.

David truly believes that the home is a living being and should be treated as such. "You will never graduate from your design. You will always continue to evolve. As long as you're living, you'll evolve, and so will your style. I like to think of the rooms that we create, the spaces that we create, as a love letter to the vision that we have for our life."

"If you're afraid of color and you want to introduce it into your home, but you don't have that commitment just yet, think small. Try it in your accessories."

David Quarles

How did you get into design?

I thought that I was going to work immediately in the world of interior design. However, during my internship evaluation, my boss told me, "Oh, you've done a great job. However, my clientele isn't used to people like you," and then she rubbed her skin. I kind of took that erroneously. I assumed the entire industry would be this way, especially in Memphis. It's a small town. So I went into corporate design for ten years before launching my design firm."

David Quarles's funky mid-century modern dining room boasts a custom hand-painted wallpaper by the designer himself. The room is layered with velvet green hairs from Joybird and anchored with a contemporary curved chandelier from French company DCWéditions.

"Fill your home with the things that represent you, things that you love, that represent your vision of life, that represent your family, that just really speak to who you are."

How does being a Black designer influence your work?

I believe we see the world just a little bit differently. Maybe see it with a little bit more hope, a little bit more joy, and that's how I create. So I pull the colors and the textures from my cultural background and really amplify that in the colors and materials that I choose to use in my designs.

How do you bring in the outdoors with your designs?

I like to look at a person's surroundings and I ask them if they have any pictures of their home or the landscape in springtime and in summer. I generally think about the studies of seasonal affective disorder (SAD), a type of depression that's related to the changes in the seasons. The landscapes from spring and summer are what I use to pull color inspiration and bring those colors into the home. It could be through a rug. It could be through chairs, through paintings. I just make sure that that color or that whole color palette is present year-round.

Do you have a design philosophy or something that you go by as a designer?

Fill your home with the things that represent you, things that you love, that represent your vision of life, that represent your family, that just really speak to who you are, and there's a curated way of doing it. Don't follow trends, because that's not you—your house should be you.

What do you want people to remember about you?

I curate from a place of joy. I want people to feel that joy in their lives, and I feel that when you have it inside of you, it spreads to others.

OPPOSITE TOP LEFT: The seating area in David's Memphis home. The mid-century console was sourced from Albany Park, and the artwork is from local Memphis artist Frances Berry Moreno. OPPOSITE TOP RIGHT: This eclectic dining room is drenched in the color Purple Rain, while the custom dining table created by Kiara Sally adds organic texture and art from Monica Lewis Art serves as a focal point. OPPOSITE BOTTOM LEFT: David's home office, designed in collaboration with Living Spaces. OPPOSITE BOTTOM RIGHT: The designer's boho chic bedroom has a whimsical plush rug from Jungalow for Loloi Rugs, modern geometric wallpaper from Chasing Paper, and a warm rattan bed.

a dream

"The use of neutrals, and the placements of more bold accents, can help create moments within a home to help carry narratives without words."

DuVäl Reynolds

An intense and strategic deep dive into the clients' wardrobe and travels is often the starting point for the illustrious and charming interiors created by DuVäl Reynolds. DuVäl prioritizes creating spaces that reflect the many layers of his clientele while focusing on the key elements of design. "I generally try to design spaces that the clients do not know that they want," DuVäl says.

To craft spaces that represent the originality that is found within each client, DuVäl keeps two key design elements at the top of his mind while designing, regardless of the client's taste and personality. "Two very simple tricks that can help any project are lighting and scale," he says. "Too often people are unaware of how proper lighting can enhance a space. This can be in the form of recessed, accent, general lighting, etc. There are so many ways to introduce moods and auras into a room just through your lighting options. Using the proper scale for a room or item can [also] make or break a space. Walking into a large room with small furniture can immediately expose poor design concepts and decisions. The same can be said for oversized pieces, which can damage traffic flow and ease of motion."

Possibly the most important part of DuVäl's process with his firm, DuVäl Design, LLC, is tapping into his clients' dreams and goals to create a space that is motivating, inspiring, and effortless.

"I always try to design, not for who the client is, but for who the client wants to be. It is my intention to create spaces that inspire the client to be and do even more than they have in the past. I believe each person is striving to be bigger and better. Our designed spaces should offer the client the hope, inspiration, and space to be just that—whatever (and whoever) they want to be!" he notes.

Cozy reading nook in the "West Coast Vintage" living room.

"Layering materials, textures, and colors can show an enhanced design concept that can feel a bit foreign to some design enthusiasts."

How does being a Black designer influence your work?

Because of my background, my culture, and my sensibilities, I approach design only from the perspective that I know, and nothing more. As a major part of my design experience, I introduce a carefree, open-door policy with clients. With many shared stories within our community, we know what it's like to be disregarded, neglected, and disrespected. Accordingly, much effort is put into creating a warm and welcoming environment and approach to clients and their projects. This, in turn, seems to offer space for genuine sincerity and candor, often opening doors to the design/personality style they actually want rather than what they think others would approve of.

Let's talk about color. How does it impact a space?

Color really *is* everything. It can convey the concept and story line without any assistance. The use of neutrals, and the placements of more bold accents, can help create moments within a home to help carry narratives without words. Using vibrant hues can create focal points and moments of interest, while duller tones can be more soothing, or even help the eye bypass areas of disinterest. Colors also offer clients the opportunity to express preferred style interpretations to guests and visitors. It is a great way to offer additional insight to one's personal brand and interests.

A Virginia living room designed by DuVäl Reynolds accentuates a uniform color palette with creams, grays, and taupes. Wood accents add subtle contrast to the space.

How do you bring in the outdoors with your designs?

The easiest and most effective way is to introduce plants. While some designers may despise the use of faux plants, I cannot express how valuable a role they can play, just by introducing the color green and lively movement. To take it a step further, be sure to use natural elements that can be found outside—like wood, stone, and even water. Textured wood and stone in surroundings can revolutionize sterile environments into warm and inviting habitats much quicker than color and pattern can. Be sure to also introduce natural colors along the way— blues, greens, browns, etc.

What do you want people to remember about you?

I hope to be remembered for effortless designs. I want each of my projects to look and feel accessible and achievable. While we put so much thought and effort into each project, we hope that our spaces look like they just "exist." We want to be remembered for creating timeless rooms that feel neither overly constructed nor manufactured.

The timeless, transitional kitchen contrasts wood cabinets with soft white cabinets and lightly textured subway tile.

For Byron Risdon, a complete room is full of layers that invite occupants to come in and stay awhile. These design layers create both interest and movement, he says. "Movement is what keeps your eye interested and engaged," Byron notes. "To incorporate movement, you can play with different hues of a particular color or use a mix of materials in a space." Specializing in calm and collected interior spaces, Byron uses soft textures and bold art to fabricate spaces that embody luxury and warmth.

His polished spaces often feature a blend of organic hues and textures, resulting in a visual harvest of life and vibrancy. His design philosophy is rooted in simplicity, but he suggests employing various tones and materials to achieve a layered and memorable space. "By using different complementary elements, you're able to take in a different view from every angle," he notes. "In every room I try to include some version of a mix of wood, metal, stone, and glass."

How do you use scale in your designs?

I want to create a natural flow and harmony in a room, and scaling everything properly is a big part of that. When designing a space, I often create an initial floor plan, agonize over it, and come back to make adjustments and sometimes a totally new plan.

Is lighting important?

Lighting is a tool for creating different moods, and being able to manipulate it to your liking can really change a space. You should have a balance of both overhead and low-level lighting. I always use dimmers so clients can decide on the mood in any room.

How do you choose the right art for a room?

You should choose pieces or objects you'll enjoy seeing on a daily basis. I believe every time you walk by a piece of art you should still appreciate it, maybe see something you hadn't before, and you should never grow tired of it.

"I incorporate functionality into my designs through pieces that are either movable or have multiple purposes."

Byron Risdon

Byron Risdon's quaint Washington, DC, apartment combines the new and old. Custom window treatments by Essence Interiors flank large windows, while the dining chairs and table are vintage pieces purchased at auction. The bar shelf is fitted with items Byron discovered during his travels in Indonesia.

Do you look for ways to achieve sustainability in your projects?

As the world grows and we continue to consume, we have to be mindful of future generations. I often prioritize using vintage and antique pieces and passing down art and accessories. We have to think outside the box and find uses for things. For example: I have repurposed a mid-century piece I bought on ebay as a tableware cupboard, bar, and, now, bath cabinet for linens.

What about functionality?

The way we see our homes has changed, and we have to create spaces that are versatile and flexible. I incorporate functionality into my designs through pieces that are either movable or have multiple purposes. Pieces like a rollaway island cart, which gives extra counter- or work space.

Does layering play a role in your designs?

I'm a firm believer in allowing a space to evolve, and evolution takes time. A well-layered room mixes finishes, materials, and styles. I'm a feeling designer; I want to create the mood and allow the design to flow from there.

Is there a trusted design tip you use often?

Paint the walls, trim, and doors the same color. It's a simple way to elevate a space, and it creates a canvas for layering other design elements.

Do you have a design philosophy?

Don't overthink it. Do what makes you feel good, because you should love the space you're in.

What do you want people to remember about you as a designer?

I want people to know me as someone who approached every project fearlessly and with a fresh perspective.

Vibrant living room inspired by the clients' love of nature.

"There's a real push and pull with different colors I'll use. Maybe on paper they don't look like they'll go well together, but when you get them in a room, they just sing!"

Brigette Romanek

Brigette Romanek found her way into a career of interior design by leaning into her passion for decorating spaces. That enjoyment she felt in designing rooms, before she was even designing for clients, is still the start of each project—it's all about feeling.

"I design 100 percent based on feel," Brigette says. "If I don't know where to start or the space isn't coming together, I go back to this—how do I want the room to feel?"

While feeling is her starting point, a surefire way to take any design to the next level, no matter where in the process, has to do with plants for Brigette. She advises, "One of the easiest ways to elevate a room is with plants. It's always resonated with me to have some sort of greenery in the house as it brings such life and energy. You can get a plant for $6 or $5,000—all of them will bring some love and light into a room. One of my go-to plants is the black olive tree. It always surprises people when they enter my living room. It makes them think a little bit differently, which I really appreciate."

From feelings to plants and everything in between, Brigette is inspired by the respect she has for her own culture to tap into her clients' backgrounds and put their stories and heritage on display.

"My story is in my soul, and it comes through in design by the moods I create," she says. "I'm so proud to be who I am, and proud of our history. I always add something personal to each family's space. Pieces that embody people's history and bring their culture into the picture make them proud and remember who they are. I love that."

How did you get into design?
It started organically and comes from a real love of what interiors can do for people. I used that passion to renovate my own home in Los Angeles after moving from London, and friends quickly took note of it and asked me to help them with their homes. I started helping a dear friend with her home in Malibu. Since I had such a love for interior design, it was a great way for me to learn. You can learn a lot before going out into the business side of design. One day, I was driving down in Malibu and just thought, *I can really do this and make a business out of it.*

Let's talk about color. How does it impact a space?
There's a real push and pull with different colors I'll use. Maybe on paper they don't look like they'll go well together, but when you get them in a room, they just sing! If it's on the walls, it can transform the room instantly. Color affects moods. My color choices all depend on the mood I'm going for, but they also must represent the person living in the space.

Why is it important to layer a room with design elements?
I want wherever your eye lands to be a special moment and something to enjoy. From the base layer (paint or wallpaper) to the final layer (accessories),

Brigette Romanek, pictured with her dog, Rufus.

The onyx bar by Roman and Williams serves as a key focal point in this Montecito, California, living room. Jan Ekselius lounge chairs are positioned in front of the bar, creating a luxe, tone-on-tone moment, while the Lindsey Adelman lighting draws the eye to the ceiling. The bold accents are paired with simple textures on the custom Charles Zana sofa and carpet from Woven.

"Texture makes a room so much more vivid and interesting, and it awakens the senses by adding dimension and feel. It can also bring things in and out of focus in a visceral way."

it all comes together to help make a room more dynamic, personal, lived-in, and cozy. The layers really bring a design home.

What about texture?
I'm a textural, tactile person. I love wools, mohairs, and different dreamy grades of velvet. Texture makes a room so much more vivid and interesting, and it awakens the senses by adding dimension and feel. It can also bring things in and out of focus in a visceral way.

Does scale play a factor in your designs?
Of course! Sometimes I play with scale with a sense of whimsy, and other times it's straightforward. I first ask, "What's the purpose of the room? What is its function?" These questions can really lay the groundwork for what I design, but whatever I choose scalewise, it must be beautiful, it must make sense for the space, and it all must be cohesive.

What about focal points?
I say to make all the pieces beautiful but make one piece the star. In different spaces the star is obviously different. It could be the rug, the sofa, a special light, etc. But I typically pick one focal point and move out from there.

Do you have a design philosophy or something that you go by as a designer?
Make it fun, unique, and most importantly, functional. My mantra—livable luxe—is constantly in my head: Will this beautiful, luxe piece be something we can use? Is it something we can enjoy? And I always say "we," because I picture myself living there! When we sit on this furniture and we entertain here, what does that feel like and how does that piece live?

What do you want people to remember about you?
I try to create spaces that are very intentional, very curated, and that lift you up. In the years to come I hope my clients remember that I brought them joy.

OPPOSITE TOP LEFT: Entryway featuring reclaimed stone floors and an 18th century fireplace mantel. OPPOSITE TOP RIGHT: In the dreamy dining room, a Martin Massé table for Kolkhoze with GamFratesi chairs for Porro, luxurious wallpaper by MJ Atelier, and a modern Thomas Newman Studio chandelier. OPPOSITE BOTTOM LEFT: Hammock by Jim Zivic. OPPOSITE BOTTOM RIGHT: Hand-painted wallpaper by MJ Atelier paired with an antique marble sink from Stone Objects.

"Adding color is one of the easiest ways to reinvent a space. New color in a room can be both transformational and transporting."

Saudah Saleem

As a mother of five, award-winning interior designer Saudah Saleem is no stranger to the importance of resilience when it comes to interior spaces. Creating livable interiors is the core of her Maryland-based design practice. Saleem employs thoughtfully placed color, texture, and pattern to create interiors that are not only charming but suited for each client's unique lifestyle.

How does color impact space?

Adding color is one of the easiest ways to reinvent a space. New color in a room can be both transformational and transporting. For instance, dark color on the walls creates a cocooning, dramatic effect, while light color creates a refreshing sense of airy calm. I love to use unexpected color combinations to create visual interest. For me, color can help push a limited space and really bring the design to life.

How can functionality impact a space?

Designing for both function and aesthetics is key. Even a pretty space can quickly get frustrating if it doesn't work for the occupants. Interiors must work well for how we live today. I love using furnishings and products that can pull double duty. For instance, washable vinyl wallpaper that looks like silk, or large, plush cocktail ottomans that also secretly house TV remotes and packs of crayons for the kids. When space is limited, every inch counts. Always look for items that fulfill more than one design or storage need. Think outside the box!

Do you have a design philosophy or something that you go by as a designer?

Through thoughtful use of color, unique accents, pattern, layered texture, and details, I design livable spaces that are inspiring, sophisticated, and soulful. I believe that you don't have to sacrifice style for functionality. Comfortable, livable, and family-friendly can go hand in hand with elegant sophistication. My designs incorporate personality and a balanced mix of function and form to create spaces that are both practical and visually appealing.

Silo Point living room designed by Saudah Saleem.

The name of Catasha Singleton's design firm—ModChic Interiors—aptly conveys the vibe of the spaces she creates. Plush rugs, dramatic wallpapers, sleek brass lighting with clean lines—each room balances modern sensibilities with sophisticated nuances. To look at her seasoned work you might get the idea that Catasha had always known she could be an interior designer, but that wasn't quite the case.

"It took a few influences in my circle of mentors to get me to believe I could absolutely pursue [interior design, but] it started out as what I'd call an innate ability," Catasha says. "I just naturally viewed spaces with my own thoughts of how things *should* look, even in a completely furnished space. The vision of recreating spaces has been with me as far back as I can remember."

The richness of Catasha's designed spaces is born from her use of varying textures: velvet chairs; artworks with organic, sculptural forms; mixed metals; and detailed wallcoverings. Paying attention to the number of textures in one space will instantly elevate the mood and comfort in a room.

"Textures are all around us and we don't even realize it," she says. "Paying attention to a wholly furnished space will show you: Once you point them out, you'll never look at a space the same again."

"I wouldn't say that specific colors make or break a space. I truly believe it's all about the overall design."

Catasha Singleton

How does being a Black designer influence your work?

I would say it's a big reason I am still going strong—through the trials and adversities, I am reminded that I have an obligation to those that look like me. And at the point I first realized that, I knew it was no longer about me, but about increasing the awareness for the culture.

OPPOSITE TOP LEFT: A modern entryway with rustic texture. OPPOSITE TOP RIGHT: A layered dining room with cool gray tones and plum velvet window treatments. OPPOSITE BOTTOM LEFT: The custom velvet sofa and accent wall transformed the builder's basic living room into a stylish conversational area. OPPOSITE BOTTOM RIGHT: Entryway with an abstract sculpture from Uttermost.

"If I can't get my ideal furnishing piece, I make sure the artwork, rugs, drapes, lighting, and/or pillows are the very best."

Let's talk about color. How does it impact a space?

For me, color is now simply a term. I think a lot of people overcomplicate it and sometimes misinterpret it. I prefer a neutral palette, but some will say, "I need more color," and in my mind, neutrals are colors, too . . . they're just neutral. Who's to say how that neutral color will change in different lights? People often underestimate the amount of color coming through from finishes, textiles, artwork, florals, and even from the view outside. At the end of the day, I wouldn't say that specific colors make or break a space. I truly believe it's all about the overall design.

What's your go-to design trick?

Accents—if I can't get my ideal furnishing piece, I make sure the artwork, rugs, drapes, lighting, and pillows are the very best.

How do you bring in the outdoors with your designs?

I'm a huge faux floral and faux plant gal. I couldn't take care of a real plant if you paid me, so I like to incorporate the most realistic-looking faux versions. I also think adding natural elements like jute rugs or even certain linen fabrics can give that outdoorsy feel. For a moody starry-sky atmosphere, I like to do dark ceilings and dim lighting.

Do you have a design philosophy or something that you go by as a designer?

If you have sought me out as a professional, you have to trust the process and trust me as the expert.

What do you want people to remember about you?

I think about this question often. How I want to be remembered drives nearly every decision I make. I want my company to be synonymous with impactful design—that we create spaces that evoke emotion.

OPPOSITE TOP: Plum velvet chairs from Bernhardt Furniture and contemporary floor lamp from Noir Furniture. OPPOSITE BOTTOM: This warm and welcoming kitchen, designed by Catasha Singleton, is shaped by soft neutrals. Black velvet barstools from Sunpan add an unexpected contrast.

Beth Diana Smith was working in corporate finance when her interest in interior design was sparked. "I wanted to redesign my home," she remembers. "I wanted to change what I did when I was twenty-three years old to be more reflective of who I was at the time, which was closer to thirty years old." To determine what a well-designed space might look like, Beth dove into research, seeking out print and online articles and blogs to learn more about design. "Somewhere in that process, the interior design bug bit me," she says.

Now a seasoned pro in the industry, Beth uses her maximalist sensibilities to create designs that are sophisticated yet bold, making sure the floor plan is rock solid before anything else. Spatial planning is the root of her design philosophy and the guiding force behind every decision that follows.

"My goal as a designer is to have the client see another realm of possibility in how they can live," Beth says. "So I spend a lot of time floor and space planning (the cake) before I even delve into furnishings (the icing)."

"As a maximalist, I believe in having various focal points. No matter where someone is in the space there is something to grab their attention or set the tone."

Beth Diana Smith

How does being a Black designer influence your work?
Being Black is the foundation of who I am, and who I am is always going to be seen in my work. Design is an intimate process, so in every space that I design, you'll see my footprint somewhere—even if it's in the smallest detail. Our Blackness is not merely a color, it's a culture, and that culture influences how I visualize a space, how I layer colors and patterns, and it's a significant part of what inspires me and what I allow to inspire me.

Let's talk about color. How does it impact a space?
Color is something that I love to use. Color can be used to brighten or dim a space, make it feel bigger or smaller, or to tell a story. It's extremely impactful and how we use it can transform a space.

A transitional kitchen remodel with mid-century hints and pops of texture. Beth Diana Smith created distinction with a two-tone peninsula and colorful art from the homeowner's collection.

Beth Diana Smith's New Jersey living room. The walls are Benjamin Moore Classic Gray, the Bungalow 5 sofa is reupholstered in a lustrous violet velvet from Fabricut. Accents include table lamps from Mitzi and Green Circles Art by Virginia Beshears.

"Layering makes a room feel curated and thoughtful. This is important because design is about the details, and it takes time to curate details. Layering can also make a room 'feel' good, especially when layered with things you love."

Why is it important to layer a room?

Layering makes a room feel curated and thoughtful. This is important because design is about the details, and it takes time to curate details. Layering can also make a room feel good, especially when layered with things you love, whether they be specific items or through the use of color and pattern.

What's your go-to design trick?

Do it in threes: Instead of using an item in a pair, use it in a trio for a bolder effect.

What about texture?

Texture brings warmth and comfortability to a space, even in a neutral palette. Texture is a must-have in every room I design.

How do you get to know clients and their lives to design their space?

I start with my client questionnaire for some basic and also detailed information; this also acts as a jumping-off point. But to really understand them and how they dream of living at home, I either have one of two approaches depending on their personality—to ask questions, or to be quiet and listen. Some people are very open and others are not. My job is to determine which they are and fit my discovery of them into what would be most comfortable for them.

Does scale play a factor in your designs?

Absolutely. The starting point for every design is to do the floor plan so I know the scale of all of the pieces. And once that starts to develop, I move to doing the same with elevations so I can ensure the pieces fit together well, proportionately in the space, and flow the way I want them to in the room.

What about focal points?

As a maximalist, I believe in having various focal points. This depends on where the room will be entered, and where the seating is, so no matter where someone is in the space, there is something to grab their attention or set the tone.

What do you want people to remember about you?

How my designs made them feel. And if we've met in person, I hope I made them feel inspired or seen, or that I at least made them laugh.

The dining room in Beth Diana Smith's townhome is anchored with a berry rug from Loloi. Custom upholstered chairs in a Calico fabric continue the eclectic aesthetic found throughout the home.

> *"When you want the option to soften the atmosphere for watching your favorite movie, consider installing dimming technology in your lighting."*

Keita Turner

For Keita Turner, interior design is a tool to promote inspiration and peace of mind in the homes and commercial spaces she designs. She says, "My mission is to create high-end residential and commercial environments that are clean and functional, warm and inviting, suitable and inspirational, but most importantly that uplift the human spirit."

Keita is all about suitability. She aims to produce interiors characterized by a confident, chic, and timeless elegance, but not confined to a particular look. "I often incorporate a harmonious, smart, tailored, thoughtful, and visually stimulating mix of natural subtle tones with deliciously vibrant accents, from divergent rough-hewn organic surfaces to glamorously translucent finishes, and use high-quality contemporary furnishings and fabrics combined with antique, vintage, and architectural pieces."

Keita also abides by a simple but effective design strategy: "Don't be afraid to mix unconventional color combinations, patterns, textures, finishes, and furnishing styles authentic to or attributed to different eras. You'll be surprised how well it works and makes for a more interesting, layered interior."

How did you get into design?

For as long as I can remember, I was enamored of my mother's copies of *Vogue* and *Architectural Digest*. My grade school teachers noted how I created my own magazines of notebook paper and distributed them to classmates. By the time I was a high school student, I was driving to a neighboring district high school—in the mornings before my regular school day began—to attend an honors art class. My art teacher encouraged me to apply to the Rhode Island School of Design. After graduating from RISD, I moved to New York City to pursue a career in the fashion industry. Several years after establishing myself as a successful fashion designer in a very cutthroat industry, I decided I needed a major change in my profession and lifestyle. I made the transition to interior design by studying at the School of Visual Arts and at Pratt Institute. After working with my mother's interior design studio, Betty R. Turner Interiors, in Saint Louis, Missouri, I struck out on my own. I have since gone on to make a name for myself as a New York City–based residential and commercial interior designer, as well as the creative director of Livvy & Neva, my own collection of vintage pillows for the home.

Let's talk about color. How does it impact a space?

People react differently to colors. Where one may find a particular color depressing and demotivating, or intense and threatening, another may find it comforting and motivating, or inspiring and heartening. I first learned how to "see" color through my mother's tutelage. My mother, Betty Toler Turner, a classically educated and trained fine artist, painter, printmaker, and sculptor, taught me how to choose and use color naturally. She explained how artists recreate commonly used color combinations in an unexpected way. By approaching my use of color using this same

Keita Turner, photographed in the 1960s Brooklyn co-op designed for Cassandra Bromfield.

"I love introducing atmosphere and mood-enhancing colors into my interiors from the endless combinations and possibilities nature provides."

philosophy, I really think about the colors found in nature and how they coexist harmoniously, and then I translate that vision into an interior space. I love introducing atmosphere and mood-enhancing colors into my interiors from the endless combinations and possibilities nature provides.

What about texture?
Harnessing tactile texture (sense of touch) and/or visual texture (sense of sight) in a space can enhance and bring dimensionality to interiors in unimaginable ways. Playing with the interconnectedness of various textural categories, such as rough and smooth, dull and shiny, hard and soft, bumpy and flat, and combining these surface qualities with other elements of interior design will produce transformative results.

How does balance impact a space?
Achieving balance in a room is the very basis of creating visually stunning interiors. Balance is accomplished by artfully distributing the visual weight of objects within a space to attain a sense of equilibrium. It can be achieved by using symmetrical, asymmetrical, and radial settings. Without visual stability, interiors will feel and look uncomfortably awkward. An unbalanced room will immediately feel off, but a balanced space will have a harmonious atmosphere. Juxtaposing lighter colored, textured items against

Cassandra Bromfield's dining room is an original, designed by the artist herself. Keita completed the room with a vintage dining table and a vintage light diffuser, which was customized in collaboration with O'Lampia Studio.

darker ones of similar shape and size will give you the desired visual weight within a room. I believe every room needs something either black or dark blue to balance and ground the space. This can be achieved by using bronze oil-rubbed door hardware, drapery rods, picture framing, or accessories.

How does lighting impact a space?

In addition to altering the mood of a room, good lighting can transform a room both configurationally and spatially. I utilize the three distinct layers of lighting together: ambient, accent, and task lighting to brighten up or soften the atmosphere in a space. Ambient lighting, or *general lighting*, provides a room's overall illumination and is generally created by using overhead light fixtures like chandeliers, semi-flush or flush mounts, pendants, ceiling fans, and recessed lights. Accent lighting, or *decorative lighting*, such as track lighting, pivotal recessed spotlights, wall sconces, uplighting, and tape lighting installed in coves, helps draw attention to prominent architectural details, impressive artwork, and other features in a home that need highlighting. Task lighting supplies illumination for specific tasks, such as cooking, reading, studying, and working—for example, bathroom vanity lights, under-cabinet lights, kitchen pendant lights, table and floor lamps, and desk lamps.

When you want the option to soften the atmosphere for watching your favorite movie, consider installing dimming technology in your lighting. Dimmers also help reduce energy consumption and save money.

How can art be powerful in a space?

I find any home that is devoid of art on walls or sculptures displayed on surfaces feels rather unwelcoming and unappealing. Artwork, large or small, alone or as part of a gallery wall, gives dimension and abundance to a room and makes it feel more personal.

When planning where to hang your art, carefully consider placement in relation to spatial furniture plans and sight lines from adjacent rooms, hallways, sitting areas, etc. Also, do not minimize the power of a well-framed original artwork. In fact, many custom frames are works of art themselves—and deserve to be seen as such. The frame is like the mother holding its child. However, art is not only confined to framed works on canvas or paper. A bold, colorful, artist-commissioned wall mural featured in a dining room could serve as a remarkable and one-of-a-kind, site-specific art installation.

Do you have a design philosophy?

I am an interior designer whose business is about creating enduring and fashionably classic designs that are beautiful, transformative, well-appointed, and orderly safe havens. My background as a former fashion designer also plays a vital role in how I approach interior design. I address interior design in a similar manner to creating a fashion collection. Silhouette, line, color and value, texture, proportion and scale, balance, unity and harmony, rhythm, and emphasis are all key elements and principles to my design process.

What do you want people to remember about you?

I want to be remembered as a citizen of the world who helped make people's lives more spiritually abundant, enriched, and productive. I would love for people to know that I did the best I could with what I was given and with what I set out to accomplish during my time here on God's green earth. I would like to be thought of as both a lover and practitioner of good design who did her best to persevere and succeed in an industry that has historically and perhaps willfully failed to recognize Black design practitioners.

OPPOSITE TOP AND BOTTOM LEFT, BOTTOM RIGHT: A Showhouse vignette features luxury printed wallpaper from Thibaut, artwork from LeftBank Art, and accessories from Waterford, Baccarat, Tiffany & Co., and Gorham. OPPOSITE TOP RIGHT: A custom walnut media shelf paired with a vintage sewing chair sourced and reupholstered by Keita.

"I design window treatments that are light and not heavy, allowing them to be fully opened, so plants and flowers can come into the space."

Lisa Turner

For as long as she can remember, Lisa Turner has had a deep admiration for all things related to art. As a young girl she would often complete do-it-yourself projects in her spare time. Her love for artistic projects and her natural gravitation to interiors would lead to over thirty years of experience and impact in the interior design community.

Lisa leads the Beverly Hills, California, based design firm Interior Obsession, where she has been creating luxe interior residential and commercial spaces since 1989.

"I forged my own signature style and legacy, welcoming livable appeal, attention to detail, and respect for the architecture," Lisa says. She remembers back when she started her firm that the number of Black interior designers was even slimmer than it is today—and it was harder to get exposure and develop a client base before the advent of social media and the Internet.

How did you get into design?
I'm an LA native and started loving the arts at a very young age. Very early on I homed in on my artistic talents and was always crafty, known as the DIY kid before DIY was popular. I began perfecting my skills as I began decorating the homes of my friends and family. After trying several other careers, I decided to go back to school and pursue a career in interior design at the Fashion Institute of Design & Merchandising, in Los Angeles, where I found my love for design and have never looked back.

How does being a Black designer influence your work?
My business and work are influenced by my culture, struggles, and the fight to be recognized. It's not that my work reflects that I'm a Black interior designer, but my struggles and business do. Black designers make up less than 2 percent of the interior

This Los Angeles seating area features disappearing sliding doors, creating ease of access to the exterior oasis.

"Color is universal as music is; color can move you just the same way as music does. It can give you a rush of excitement, change your mood and energy level."

design field. The struggle is real and has been for decades. I started as a designer before the Internet and social media and, basically, we were only a handful at that time.

What's your go-to design trick?
It starts in the very beginning of the design phase: space planning and thinking about the function of space. If the room does not function and the layout is not correct, I don't care how beautiful the design is, it is a failure. I have always been good with scale and relationships in space, flow, and focal points. It is the starting point to any good design.

How do you bring the outdoors into your designs?
Designing past the four walls, seeing through the windows and doors out into gardens, patios, side yards, and backyards to expand the space and overall serenity of the home. Being surrounded with nature impacts health and overall well-being. Nature makes you feel better and comfortable, and I design window treatments that are light and not heavy, allowing them to be fully opened, so plants and flowers can come into the space.

How do you get to know clients and their lives to design their space?
My design approach is to be a good listener, observing and looking at reactions from our one-on-one conversation about what they love, what they dislike, how they want to live in the home, and what's important.

What do you want people to remember about you?
That I was a pioneer in the world of design. I formed the first Black interior design organization, The Society of African American Interior Designers, in the early 1990s, along with Beverly Miller, setting out to find people of color in the industry, with a goal of making their names known. Today, I continue the fight for our people in the industry.

An electric blue music room designed for and inspired by the legendary Stevie Wonder.

Designing for New York homes and apartments can be daunting due to limitations of space, lighting, and access to nature. But those kinds of projects are Alvin Wayne's bread and butter. He has mastered the art of designing such spaces by creating luxurious and functional rooms that are teeming with strategically selected colors, patterns, and furnishings. "I tend to lean towards colors that you see in nature," Alvin says. "I still like the space to feel calm and modern, with a clean look, while using nature-inspired colors that you would see when looking outside at the world."

A core principle for Alvin is that the home should be a collection of things that bring the homeowner joy. His use of texture and scale produces intimate spaces with tons of personality. "Texture is everything. I use texture from the rugs to the duvet cover. I even use texture on the walls. If your wallpaper has a print, that's a visual texture." He adds, "I love layering. That's when personality comes into play. That's when a room gets its true personality."

"As long as the scales and sizes of the patterns are different, you can mix patterns that have similar colors in them."

Alvin Wayne

How do you use color in your designs?
Color often sets the tone for the space. It's all about the mood. Whatever color you choose or gravitate towards, it sets the aesthetic of the space. In addition to natural colors, I also use black and white a lot because they ground the space. I then infuse color into my spaces through accessories, wallpaper, and pattern play.

How about lighting?
Lighting is extremely important since it can really set the mood. I think it's important to use sconces, lamps, and also overhead lighting. If you're in a rental and you have a kitchen light you don't love, swap it out for something fabulous. Incorporating task lighting where you can is also a great way to maximize the lighting in your home.

A bold botanical wallpaper from Prestige Wallcoverings is paired with vintage aesthetic plates from Fornasetti in Alvin Wayne's New York dining room.

"Don't be afraid to play with outside materials or outdoor fabrics and use them inside as performance fabrics."

How do you utilize patterns?

When you use a pattern, play with the scale. As long as the scales and sizes of the patterns are different, you can mix patterns that have similar colors in them. If you pull one color out of one pattern and it is repeated in another pattern, but the sizes are different, it'll always work.

How important is art in a space?

I'm a firm believer that art is very subjective. Art is something that the homeowners should really feel moved by. They should really be in love with it. The best use of art is to really put it on display. It can be a singular piece or you can have a gallery wall.

What about sustainability? Does that play a role in your designs?

I incorporate sustainability by using a lot of products that are found in nature and that can be replenished like marble and wood. I also use low-VOC paint (paint with low volatile organic compounds).

How is movement interpreted in a space?

Movement for me is related to the furniture plan. How is your house laid out? What is the path that you're going to take? How are you directing me through your space? It's important for me to find out how you live and how you navigate through your space, and then incorporate furniture so that it supports your movement through the space.

Do you have a trusted design tip you use often?

For the sofa, I have a maximum of three throw pillows. I feel like the sofa you spent money on is a great sofa, so you don't need to hide it with a bunch of pillows. So three pillows: two on one end, one on the other one. That's enough.

What is your design philosophy?

My design philosophy, and probably my life philosophy, is that everybody deserves to live in luxury, no matter the budget. Luxury is attainable.

OPPOSITE TOP: A Lower East Side living room in classic black and white texture with organic accents. OPPOSITE BOTTOM: The intimate primary bedroom is balanced with a deep graphic wallpaper from Belarte Studio, finished with the leather Maraba bed and Kamet duvet from CB2.

Calm and cozy living room
with an abstract canvas
from art by R.A.W.

"Bold colors can set the tone for creating memories, while softer tones can bring much-needed calm after a long day."

Eneia White

For Queens, New York, based interior designer Eneia White, her design profession was a serendipitous discovery made while studying at the Art Institute of Washington. "I didn't know interior design was an occupation possibility until I saw a TV show one day of a home being remodeled," Eneia says. "I looked into it and enrolled as an interior design major the following semester!"

Living in and designing spaces across the United States, Eneia has gained an appreciation for and understanding of the robust cultural preferences some clients focus on. By paying close attention to these passions, Eneia creates soothing, deeply personal designs—like the wall display she installed for a client's coveted sneaker collection.

"I love a good wild card or plot twist moment," she says. "I always try to use an ordinary object in a very nonordinary way—but make it classic."

How does being a Black designer influence your work?
"The same, but different" comes to mind. We, as people, come from a variety of backgrounds, and yet we are all the same, but different. I bring this into each project, blending timeless elements with something unique, something just for the client: Later, it might be copied or duplicated, but they will forever be the first to have it.

Let's talk about color. How does it impact a space?
Color is the first thing we notice about a room; everything else is secondary! Bold colors can set the tone for creating memories, while softer tones can bring much-needed calm after a long day.

Why is it important to layer a room design?
Layering is important for timeless and well-received spaces. I've found that clients are more willing to take a risk or try something new—whether materials or style—when they see it woven into a well-balanced room.

Brooklyn townhome with a custom bookshelf designed by Eneia White.

What about texture?

Texture is the savior in a room full of neutrals! For clients who love toned-down color palettes, we turn up the texture. Textured wallpaper is one of our favorite ways to shake things up a bit.

How do you bring in the outdoors with your designs?

In a city like New York, sometimes the concrete jungle is the only outdoor experience. We love creating custom art inspired by a client's outdoor travels, and oversized photography is also a fan favorite.

How do you get to know clients and their lives to begin creating their space?

Early in the design process, we arrange three palettes of physical samples so that clients can see and touch the materials. We note their favorites, and often their choices surprise them. This leads to opportunity; we can embrace colors and trends that we are all excited to try.

What about focal points?

I generally create multiple focal points. This feels more organic, as if the space was created over time. If I have one wow-element, I support it with symmetry and calm tones to keep the space easy to live in.

Do you have a design philosophy?

Pink is a neutral.

What do you want people to remember about you?

My ability to tell a story without words: I love the storytelling behind interior design. Every client's space tells a unique story of memories, hopes, and the times they spent there. I love being a part of that.

Soft white window treatments effortlessly filter light in this easy-going living room with muted layers and velvety texture.

"A well-designed room should have a bold yet balanced use of color. There isn't a color I'd shy away from when designing a space. The key is balance."

Nicole White

At the start of Nicole White's design career, she was a reporter by day, only pursuing her passion for design during the evenings and weekends. Now that she's pursuing design full-time, Nicole carries her journalism experience with her as she tackles new projects. "I know that I lean in to my reporting skills when designing because I'm truly trying to tell a story," Nicole says. "During the consultation, I'm asking a lot of questions, not just about the clients' design needs, but about who and what inspires them."

The Jamaican-born designer often infuses heavy Caribbean inspiration into her projects. "I've always used bold colors and textures like burlap and linen throughout my design, because it's what I saw growing up in the islands. It's been important to me as a designer to never hide who I am and be proud to showcase my voice throughout my designs," she notes.

Nicole believes a space should be filled with elegant details for maximum impact. "I want to see and feel different textures—the soft touch of a velvet throw pillow next to a leather pillow with a fringe detail is exquisite to see and touch. It also adds dimension, which is key in any well-designed room."

Why is it important to layer a room?

In addition to being a storyteller, I'm a fashionista at heart, and so I also approach the design of a space as I would when getting dressed. There are the fundamental elements—the furniture, rugs, lighting—and then we need to elevate the outfit from there. Do we add a head wrap—for the space, maybe a Juju hat? How many rings, bracelets, and necklaces do I feel like rocking today—for the space, beaded necklaces and sculptures? Will our window treatments be casual, or will we add luxurious trim details to make them really soar? All these well-placed layers can take a space from being just good to extraordinary.

This bold office is outfitted with contrasting black walls and a white ceiling while a daring pink velvet and multicolored patterns create a layer of fun.

"There's fun and fantasy when we use patterns and contrast to impact a space. The trick is to not be afraid to try, to step outside of your comfort zone and have fun."

How important is lighting in a space?

Lighting is one of the most important and yet overlooked aspects of design. There's functional lighting—like a flush-mounted fixture overhead or recessed lights. But it's also important to include other layers of lighting—sconces, pendants, and table and floor lamps for specific areas in a space. The most important thing we believe is to have all lights on dimmers when possible. Nothing beats the ability to dim a light as needed to control the lighting and mood you want to feel in a space.

Any tips for incorporating art in the home?

Take your time when curating your art collection. It should really speak to your soul, and not just be something you purchased to fill a wall. Find artists you like and purchase a print if you can't afford an original piece. Find art that brings you joy, that makes you smile when you see it because it reminds you of why or where you purchased it. Art is like living with another soul in a space, so curate that energy as carefully as you would any relationship. Also, install art as it speaks to you, not as someone on Pinterest tells you it should be.

How do you create balance in a room?

One of the biggest lessons in design is that balance does not mean symmetry. We do not need matching nightstands, end tables, or table lamps on both ends of a console to achieve balance in a space. We need to be sure there is equal or somewhat equal weight in a space. This allows us to stand in the space and appreciate each detail without feeling like something is missing or overlooked. An easy way to do this on a foyer console is to install a lamp on one side, with a stack of books and a vase with flowers on the other side. The table will feel balanced, but not repetitive.

Do you have a design philosophy you go by?

I always design all spaces with these premises: "What if?" and "Why not?" I also believe design should truly reflect a client's personality. You should walk into someone's home, office, or restaurant and say, "Yes! This space belongs to so-and-so."

What do you want people to remember about you as a designer?

I want to be remembered as a self-taught designer who worked on her craft quietly over the years, built her confidence with each project, and then embraced her talent and passion and stepped boldly into her purpose. I want to be remembered as someone who was always honest about her journey, as someone who mentored young designers along the way and offered them a helping hand, because I know well the sting of not having anyone to turn to in those early and uncertain years.

OPPOSITE TOP AND BOTTOM LEFT, BOTTOM RIGHT: Details in a Ritz Carlton private residence in Coconut Grove, Miami. OPPOSITE TOP RIGHT: A fearless orange sofa, perfect for lounging, in Nicole White's home office.

The grand modern conversation
area in a Ritz Carlton private
residence in Coconut Grove, Miami.

"Humans are tactile, and color and texture add soulfulness to our living spaces. Color and texture are our friends."

Joy Williams

Joy Williams begins her creative process by digging deep to discover what brings her clients joy and how she can tap into that feeling and design their homes around it. To accomplish this effect, Joy ends up focusing often on crafting art-forward interiors at her firm, Joyful Designs Studio.

"I believe that how you choose to experience your home can be an artful expression of self," Joy says. "I love helping our clients achieve such a deeply personal home experience, and a large part of that is in the art we help them choose for their spaces."

Design pillars at Joy's design studio include eye-catching patterns and saturated colors. "I love bold geometric patterns, but also have an affinity for folksy and culturally impactful ones. I also lean towards saturated color and wallpaper or wallcoverings."

Homes designed by Joy are centered in sustainability and wellness. "We love a vintage mix to add soul, provenance, and gravity to a space. We often practice sustainable principles by incorporating refurbished and vintage furniture and decor in our designs. And we shop with trade partners who also abide by principles of sustainability. We aren't fans of fast furniture trends, and we place high value on heritage-quality furniture when sourcing for our clients."

How do you bring in the outdoors with your designs?

Biophilic design is important to our ethos and to how we design spaces for our clients. Fresh and clean air and nontoxic living environments have never been more important than they are today. Plant life and using living, breathable fabrics are key elements of our design approach to sustainability and a healthy home mantra. One plant, five plants, thirty plants—you can never have too many.

Joy Williams incorporates a custom ebony desk, a striking wall mural from Minted, patterned ottomans from West Elm, and a stunning Bisa Butler print in her home office.

"Plant life and using living, breathable fabrics are key elements of our design approach to sustainability and a healthy home mantra."

What about color?

Color changes everything. Even the absence of color can have an impact on a space. The color spectrum is so vast, and there's room for all manner of gradients and shades. I use color to express joy, mood, and remembrance of place in my designs. In the absence of color, I will use high contrast and texture to add volume and interest to a space. Humans are tactile, and color and texture add soulfulness to our living spaces. Color and texture are our friends. Use them liberally.

How do you feel about using focal points?

Not every room allows for a focal point. It truly depends on the space. Most focal points tend to primarily involve an accent wall, which, in my opinion, tends to be overdone. If you can, create organic focal points with substantive architectural elements in a space. Adding more architecturally significant elements leads to less obtrusive or trendy focal points that you will inevitably tire of, especially when they are a feature in everyone else's home.

How important is lighting?

Lighting is critical. My preference has always been for southern-facing natural light and minimum coverage on windows. At dusk, I prefer soft, secondary indirect lighting via lamps and sconces. I know statement chandeliers are loved by all, but I really use them as jewelry pieces in a space. I don't want to see them turned on unless there's a party or entertaining happening in a space.

Do you have a design philosophy?

Great design is a feeling, and your home should reflect a sense of joy, curiosity, and wellness when you enter it.

What do you want people to remember about you as a designer?

I hope people remember my *joie de vivre*, my friendship, love, and kindness. All the things that strengthen me through Christ. All the things I learned at my mother's knee.

Hallway vignette from the Adler on the Park Showhouse. Joy Williams was inspired by her travels to Kyoto, Japan, and her love of West African design. The space boasts a custom credenza designed by Joy.

"Art is pivotal in a space. It's essential to understand that expensive art isn't necessarily good art."

Ron Woodson

There is hardly an interior design–related publication or platform that has not amplified the presence of Ron Woodson, cofounder of Woodson and Rummerfield's House of Design in Los Angeles. Ron, the son of a jazz musician, had a rich and creative childhood, which is integrated into each and every room designed by him. In addition to innumerable accolades, his affinity for culture and architecture has birthed the Save Iconic Architecture preservation organization.

Many of Ron's design projects are brimming with art from some of the greatest artists to ever live. Clients are often attracted to Woodson and Rummerfield's House of Design because of the ingenious showcasing of art they have been able to forge for clients. "I designed a custom velvet emerald green serpent-shaped sofa so that anywhere you sit in the room, you're able to view the art," Ron says.

Rooms that are designed by Ron can typically be described as opulent, artful, and classic. "Understanding how to think outside of the box while keeping the clients' needs at the forefront is always the ultimate goal."

How does being a Black designer influence your work?

I'm on panels all the time and I speak on diversity and inclusion in the design industry, which we are still lacking on several levels. When my career began, my only intention was to do really good design. The majority of my clients over the years have been very wealthy white clients, but I didn't let that deter me.

It wasn't until I had been doing this for a good period of time that I thought, *There needs to be more people who look like me in this industry.* There were younger designers who were coming up behind me, who actually looked to me as a mentor and who saw there were other Black designers, so I felt

This striking Hollywood glam foyer includes artwork by Andy Warhol, a vintage original 1940s Lucite and brass railing, and a stair runner ("Climbing Leopard") by Diane von Furstenberg.

This Ritz Carlton Residence
at L.A. Live has custom
stone floors designed by
Woodson and Rummerfield,
a Minotti Los Angeles leather
sectional, chandeliers by
Tony Duquette from Nanz,
French dining chairs from the
1940s, a hand painted
mirror, and drapery panels
in a rich Pierre Frey fabric.

"In larger rooms, try incorporating various seating areas, not just one seating area to encompass a whole room. Having various conversation areas in a room, based on the scale of the room, is very warm, inviting to the eye."

like I could do this. I thought it was my obligation at this point to be a beacon of hope and inspiration for the younger generation of Black designers. So that is what I hold dear to my being Black—helping others like me.

What's your go-to design trick?

If you have a smaller room that has nice light and windows, to make that room feel larger take the window treatments from the ceiling to floor. It's a trick to the eye and it makes the room feel large even if it isn't.

How important is it to incorporate art into a space?

Art is pivotal in a space. It's essential to understand that expensive art isn't necessarily good art. There's a lot of great up-and-coming artists who just need a shot, but have and do wonderful, wonderful work. Another important note: Art does not need to "match" the room. I work from the perspective of the art, and what it says, and what it says for the room, and what it says about the client. Art really speaks to the inhabitants of the home. I've designed rooms around a piece of art before, but as I said, I don't pick the art to match the room.

What about scale?

When you walk into a room—let's just say it's a large room—you must understand how to make that room human scale, and that comes from really understanding perspective and scale. In larger rooms, try incorporating various seating areas, not just one seating area to encompass a whole room. Having various conversation areas in a room, based on the scale of the room, is very warm, inviting to the eye. Take full advantage of the scale of the interior of a room. A sofa or chairs do not have to be against the wall, for example.

Having ample egress around a room is important, but having it be really welcoming when you walk into the room is too, so you really want to just lounge and feel comfortable in the space. The scale of a room and how it's designed is extremely important for that.

Do you have a design philosophy or something that you go by as a designer?

My design philosophy is to make the world a more beautiful place. I have clients all over the world, and that has been my goal. That's my philosophy: to make the world a more beautiful place, one project at a time.

What do you want people to remember about you?

I want to bring beauty to the world. Also, I want to be remembered for being an advocate of good design and an advocate for helping and bringing the next generation of people of color behind me to the forefront in this great industry.

OPPOSITE TOP: Ron Woodson, photographed in a Hollywood Hills living room. The art is from Wendover and the stone urn and frog chair are from Michael Taylor. OPPOSITE BOTTOM: A Century City penthouse living room with a custom sofa by Woodson and Rummerfield.

Acknowledgments

A huge thank you to all of our designers who contributed to this book. I'm honored to share your stories, to continue to amplify your voices within the industry, and to create more visibility of the artistry around the world for those who share our experiences.

To the many photographers who eagerly permitted the use of your images, I am forever grateful. I celebrate you in this moment along with the designers. This book is only possible because of you and your immense talent.

Doug Turshen, I owe you so many thanks for presenting such an amazing opportunity to me and the organization. Steve Turner, thank you for your hard work until the very last minute in curating the graphic elements for this book. Kelli Kehler, your guidance and contributions throughout this entire process were truly invaluable to the completion of this project. I literally could not have done this without you. Lizzy Hyland, the support you provided was a breath of fresh air when I was faced with challenges while securing the content that graces these pages. Latriece, thank you for your dedication, late night hours, thousands of phone calls, emails, and Instagram DMs. For my editor, Shawna Mullen, and the entire Abrams team, I cannot thank you enough for believing in my vision from the start. Thank you all for understanding the importance of a book like this and your expertise and guidance at every stage. Thank you all for being there throughout this journey.

Keia McSwain, the mentorship and friendship we have built have been rewarding in more ways than one. Thank you for being a confidant without judgment or pacification. Your encouragement, wisdom, and prayers have allowed me to flourish both personally and professionally.

Brendan and Kayla, I thank you for your guidance and expertise during the many ups and downs of this process. The creativity and knowledge you bring to all of our projects, events, and partnerships are priceless.

Amy Astley, thank you for your continued support and believing in our mission. I am truly grateful for your willingness to step up and elevate our endeavors, big or small.

To our late mentor and mother of the movement, Kimberly Ward: Gratitude does not feel like a large enough word to describe my appreciation for your ability to see in me what I could not see in myself. Thank you for trusting me to expand on your dreams.

For my amazing friends, sisters, and cousins: Thank you for always celebrating my every accomplishment, no matter how small. Thank you for the reminders of days past whenever I felt fear or uncertainty when faced with a new opportunity. Thank you for the random scriptures, encouraging words, and much needed laughter on the days I needed them most.

Mama, thank you for encouraging and supporting me through all of my exploration over the years. It's because of you that I choose courage and take on every opportunity that I'm presented with, even when I don't feel qualified. Dad, thank you for instilling in me from a young age the value of hard work and my ability to make my dreams a reality. The many lessons you taught me when you thought I wasn't listening are the fuel behind me pursuing my passions.

To my grandparents Betty, June, and Lawrence, who helped raise me, watched over me during the summer, and cultivated my love for stories and the importance of understanding our history.

To my husband and partner, I could never thank you enough for the unconditional love, support, and encouragement you have given me for the past thirteen years.

To all of the readers, thank you from the bottom of my heart for supporting our mission. I hope that you've learned many things and have come to know and love the featured designers as I have.

Photo Credits

Front cover: *Woman and Flowers IV* by Danilo de Alexandria

Back cover: Yoshihiro Makino, *Architectural Digest* © Condé Nast featuring artwork *Prima Facie (Fifth State): Avant Garde*, © John Baldessari, 2007, courtesy Estate of John Baldessari © 2023 and courtesy Sprüth Magers. Ink-jet print mounted on aluminum; enamel paint on canvas, 52½ × 84" (133.4 × 213.4 cm) overall dimensions. Photograph also features artwork by D'lisa Creager

2, 192–193, 198–199: Douglas Friedman/Trunk Archive

4: Marco Ricca

7, 71, 75, 255: Winnie Au

9: Stephanie Ferguson

10: Marie Thomas

11,13: Marc Mauldin Photography, Inc.

14: Julien Drach

15–17, 19: Francis Amiand

21: Jesse Volk

22: Phylicia J. L. Munn

23: Justina Blakeney

25: Roberto Garcia Photography

26, 28–29, 31, 33–35: Justina Blakeney

27: Jenna Ohnemus Peffley

36: Ferrell Phelps

37: Laurie Perez

39–41: Aaron Dougherty

42: Pippa Drummond

45–47, 51 *(top, bottom right)*: Brittany Ambridge

48–49, 51 *(bottom left)*: David A. Land/OTTO

52: John Konkal

53: Michael Wells

54–55: Domonique Vorillion

57: Ethan Tweedie Photography

59: Norell Giancana

60–61: Neue Focus

63: Mike Kelley

64–67, 69: Janelle Gokule

70: Sharon Shu

72–73: Anthony Dunning

76: Hilary Jean

77: Jana Davis Pearl *(top)*, Bess Friday *(bottom)*

78: Andrew Michael Phillips

81: David Christensen

82–83, 106: Kimberly Murray

84, 86–87: Nick McGinn of Nick McGinn Photography

88–89: Robert Clark

90–93, 95: Brian Wetzel Photo

96: Kelli Boyd

97,99–101: William Waldron/OTTO

98: Elaine Griffin

103: Joshua McHugh

105: Danielle Finney

107,109: Mecca Gamble McConnell

110–113, 115: Lauren Pressey

116: Cat Harper Photography

117: Jeff Herr Photo

118–119, 121: Andre Hilton

122, 123 *(top)*: Jennifer Hughes

123 *(bottom)*: Jenn Verrier

124: Kendrick Terrell

125, 127: Ryan Garvin

129: Nathan Schroder

130–133: Werner Straube Photography

134, 135 *(bottom)*: Stephan Speranza

135 *(top)*: David Patterson

136: Jessica Neste

137–139, 224, 227–233: Nick Glimenakis

141: Brian W. Fraser, Bailey, Orange, NJ, 2018

143: Michael London

144–147, 149: Venjhamin Reyes

150: Monique Floyd

152–153: Laura Sumrak

154: Cameron Reynolds Photography

156: Amber Gluckin

157: Dare Johnson

158: Trey Thomas

161–163: Rayon Richards

164, 166–167: Chris Little, Atlanta

168, 171 *(top right, bottom left)*: Angie Choi

169: Conect

171 *(top left, bottom right)*: Nike Onile

172–173: Andrea Muscurel

174, 177 *(bottom left)*: Anthony Hardge

175, 177 *(top left)*: David Quarles

177 *(top right)*: Kimberly Thomas

177 *(bottom right)*, **178–179**: Selaviè Photography

180, 184–185: Markus Wilborn

181: Stacy Zarin Goldberg 2022

182, 183: Stylish Productions

186, 188–189, 200–202: Keyanna Bowen

187: High End Portraits/Jon Meadows

191: Ye Rin Mok

194–195, 197: Yoshihiro Makino, *Architectural Digest* © Condé Nast

203: Antar Hanif

204–205, 207 *(top)*: Colleen Scott

207 *(bottom)*: Par Bengtsson

208–211, 213: Mike Van Tassell Photography

215–217, 219 *(top right)*: Kelly Marshall/OTTO

219 *(top left, bottom left and right)*: Brad Bunyea

220–221, 223: Frank Turner III

225: Hoshi Joell

234: Donna Peplin, Owner, TYE

235, 237 *(top left, bottom left and right)*, **239:** Kris Tamburello

237 *(top right)*: Gloribell LeBron

240, 242: Pamela King

241: Michelle Linneka

244: Michael Allen

245–249: Karyn Millet

251 *(top)*: John Ellis

251 *(bottom)*: Angela Markew

253: Werner Straube Photography

254

Editor: Shawna Mullen
Design Manager: Danny Maloney
Managing Editor: Glenn Ramirez
Production Manager: Kathleen Gaffney

Book design by Doug Turshen with Steve Turner
Project Manager: Kelli Kehler
Consulting Photography Editor: Lizzy Hyland

Library of Congress Control Number: 2023930553

ISBN: 978-1-4197-6364-9
eISBN: 978-1-64700-767-6

Printed and bound in China
10 9 8 7 6 5 4 3 2 1

In 2023, the Black Interior Designers Network (BIDN) rebranded as Black Interior Designers, Inc. (BID).
The organization is listed as BIDN/BID throughout the book to represent both the legacy and current brand.

Abrams books are available at special discounts when purchased in quantity for premiums and
promotions as well as fundraising or educational use. Special editions can also be created to specification.
For details, contact specialsales@abramsbooks.com or the address below.

Abrams® is a registered trademark of Harry N. Abrams, Inc.

ABRAMS The Art of Books
195 Broadway, New York, NY 10007
abramsbooks.com

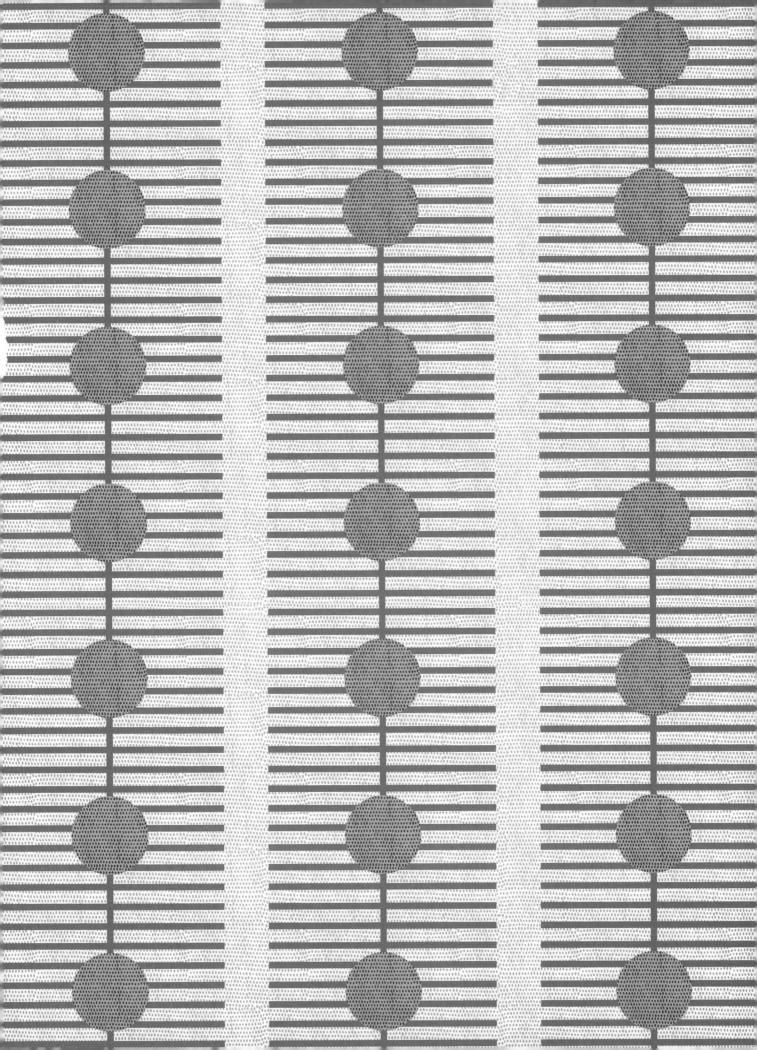